Words spoken to the heart at night
Stored and treasured for a lifetime
Finally brought to life and light

A Spiritual Odyssey

One Woman's Journey
of Faith and Fulfilment

PAULINE DOYLE

SABRESTORM
STORIES

A catalogue record for this book is available from the British Library.
Designed and typeset according to clients instructions by Sabrestorm Stories.
Published by Sabrestorm Stories Ltd,
The Olive Branch, Caen Hill, Devizes, Wiltshire SN10 1RB United Kingdom
Website: www.sabrestormstories.com
Email: enquiries@sabrestormstories.co.uk

ISBN 978-191316306-8

Dedicated to the memory of
my beloved husband Tom
who shared my life, my dreams and
many of the travels in this book

and

to our children and grandchildren
for whom this was originally compiled

Contents

PART SEVEN - God's Grace Abounds

PART EIGHT - A Different Kind of Journey

PART NINE - With Us Till the End

ACKNOWLEDGEMENTS

Grateful thanks are due to Penny and the team at Sabre-storm Stories for their encouragement, coaching and sheer belief in me and in bringing my experiences 'to life and light'.

To Ranilo Cabo, for capturing the essence of my journeys in his artwork on the front cover.

My heartfelt thanks are due firstly to my dear daughter, Anne who has worked so tirelessly side by side with me in the production of this book, offering her many words of encouragement and wisdom as well as constructive criticism along the way. Bringing her organisational skills and business acumen to the fore, she has devoted herself unreservedly to the many time-consuming tasks behind the scenes such as proofreading, editing the original manuscript, seeking permission to mention people by name in the book, applying for copyrights, dealing with correspondence and meeting deadlines. She has also helped me in finding an audience for my book. Finally, I would like to thank Anne for her patience in listening to me re-telling some of the stories until she was almost word perfect!

To my son, Stephen for checking all Scripture and other references and for being my 'Tech Support,' frequently coming to my aid when my limited computer skills bedevilled me.

To my son, Peter for the many delicious meals he thoughtfully prepared and delivered so that I could continue writing.

To my grandson, Tom for bringing me into the 21st Century by creating my website and for getting me connected on social media and my thanks to other family members too for their support in the background.

Support of various kinds came from a few friends who learned that I was writing my memoirs and followed with interest the various stages of the book's production. Of special note was the completely unexpected and very generous gift from Gemma, when we were in a critical stage of editing. Labelled 'Editing Survival Kit,' it contained many refreshing items including a bottle of champagne, which we intend to save until the ink is dry and we are finally published.

To Ricky, who first renewed my hope that the Pentecost experience is 'for real' and is 'for now' and to Peter Carty for introducing me to the Renewal Movement.

To Rev Pat Taylor for his God-given gift of healing and for his imparting of the Holy Spirit to me and many others.

To the powerful ministry and witness of Ruth Heflin who opened my eyes to the power of the Holy Spirit and showed from her life how to trust in His promptings. She first brought my attention to the plight of the Jews in Russia.

To all the members of Marconi Christian Fellowship, who

played their part in giving me a glimpse of the richness of their particular denominations. Of special memory are Alan Robertson and Peter Bettles, from whom I learned so much, to our mutual benefit.

To all my teachers and tutors, who completed my education especially in more recent times to Marguerita Gosling from the Camberley Bible Study Group, and to all who have influenced my life by their teaching and example.

Of special note are my dear parents, Martha and Jack, my first teachers in life, who showed me the importance of kindness, compassion and truthfulness.

INTRODUCTION

I knew I had to write this book! Way back in 1983, I believe I heard a message from the Lord saying,

"Thou shalt write of Me and of My work in thee. Thy pen shall flow in My word"

Unsure of what these words could mean, I stored them in my heart for many years. It was only when, several decades later, in recounting snippets about my travels to China to my grandson and his fiancée, they prompted me to write down my memoirs.

Time went by again, but it was only the enforced lockdown during the Covid pandemic which gave me the impetus, finally, to put pen to paper and to write my 'spiritual memoirs' for my children and grandchildren.

One memory led to another and in time, encouraged by family and friends who felt that the book could appeal to a wider audience, my memoirs had suddenly turned into a book! It would seem that the second part of the prophetic message, "Thy pen shall flow in My word" was becoming a reality.

ALL PART OF GOD'S PLAN

EARLY STIRRINGS
1945-1957

Where were the McGrath family going at the same time every Sunday morning? Hail, rain or shine they would make their quiet procession through the silent streets below my window. I had noticed this pattern from my observation post, head framed by raised net curtain, at the window in my parents' bedroom; parents blissfully unaware of my presence as they slept.

I did not know why it attracted me so, but I was greatly drawn to that family routine somehow. Where were they going? What was so important to them, I wondered, as they walked, slowly and purposefully, towards their destination, and I gradually became aware of this weekly pattern?

The McGrath's, I later learned, were an Irish Catholic family consisting of mum, dad, son Gerard and daughter Winifred. The children were a few years older than I was but when I eventually joined St Francis' School, I quickly learned the object of their weekly family pilgrimage. They were going to Sunday Mass!

This revelation answered my earlier intrigue but created

even more questions. Why were they the only people from our neighbourhood attending Mass? Why were we not going, too?

From the age of three to five and before the advent of 'Big School,' I had attended a Protestant Sunday School with the local children and there learned about Jesus, for which I shall be ever grateful. There, too, the seeds of my ecumenical heart were sown, an openness to different faiths. But once I started to attend day school, my mother explained that I could not attend both. For the first time I realised there was a difference between my home friends and my school friends. We were Catholic. They were not. It never occurred to me to question her further because children of my generation would not usually challenge the decision of a parent. The reason for my parents' disaffiliation was never disclosed. In their minds, it was just unthinkable to send their child to anything other than a Catholic school. To capture the mindset, the expression, "Once a Catholic, always a Catholic," comes to mind!

Midway through primary school and aged about eight, we were encouraged to develop the practice of attending Mass on Sundays, which was recorded with an extra tick against our name in the class register the next day. This was of considerable concern initially because my parents were not themselves in the habit of attending Mass. Fortunately, I was already accustomed to walking to school with a group of other children, or even taking the tram, so it was not too daunting a task for me to attempt alone the journey to church, located right next door to my school, in order to get that special tick, which became almost more important than the purpose for which I was now making my own lonely weekly pilgrimage.

How I would have valued just tagging along with the McGrath family in those earlier days! It came as no surprise to learn that the McGrath children both joined the Religious Life, Gerard as a priest and Winifred as a nun, later to become Mother Superior of her Order. It reinforces the nurture versus nature debate, doesn't it?

Still aged eight, I contracted diphtheria and was in hospital for two months, during which time I lost the use of my legs and had to learn how to walk again. I could attend neither school nor Mass for many months. By the time I returned to classes, the extra tick in the Mass Register had ceased, along with my church attendance.

The one saving grace for my faith life was when Auntie Molly, my father's sister, came to stay with us. She always went to Mass, and eventually I was able to join her. I really admired her deep faith and she became the role model I was unconsciously seeking. Much later, my father joined us and, paradoxically, it was through his occasional appearances at Mass with us that the parish priests came to hear about us as a family, after which, regular pastoral visits were made to the home. Through this contact, my mother, by that time crippled with rheumatoid arthritis, also came back to faith. But this all happened in my late teens, so had no influence on my early development. I just share this so as not to leave the question hanging in the air, "What happened to the parents?"

Not long after my recuperation from diphtheria, I distinctly remember saying to my mother one day,

"God spoke to me today, Mummy."

"Don't be silly, God doesn't speak to you," she retorted.

"But He did," I replied, most emphatically.

Known for my truthfulness (this was instilled at home and at school), she decided to take another approach.

"Well, what did He say?"

My reply would shatter her complacency, as she listened to her young child spell out the following sentence.

"You will be a missionary for Me."

Not knowing what to make of this and to avoid any possibility of my being ridiculed, she quickly instructed me never to speak of this again to anyone. I duly complied and kept this secret conversation to myself, but for a long time pondered the words, trying to make sense of them. In my limited understanding, a missionary was a priest or nun who went to foreign lands to spread the Gospel. This prompted my further query; did it mean I was to become a nun?

From the path my life took, I eventually realised there must be more than one way of becoming a missionary, but many years would pass before I would appreciate this. So, the prophecy would lie dormant until the Lord reminded me of it many years hence, in quite surprising ways.

About the age of eleven, the daughter of one of our neighbours, a young woman of about eighteen, invited me to join her for a performance of the ballet, *The Nutcracker Suite* - my first ever ballet, indeed my first experience of live entertainment apart from the circus. It was to be something I would never forget, because it was on that occasion that I sensed something 'Other.' It was the very Presence of God conveyed in the beauty of the performance and the enchanting music, which seemed to seep into the very crevices of my soul. Something was born in me that evening.

As the ballet came to a close and the applause rose up from the audience, I found myself inadvertently making the Sign of the Cross instead! I felt foolish initially but now realise that my response was, in fact, authentic and indeed most appropriate. It had been for me not merely a beautiful performance but an encounter with the Living God! He is everywhere, I reasoned, and in all things. He is beauty itself!

Whilst writing these memoirs many years later, I have only just heard the term to describe this experience; a numinous experience, which means an experience of awe and wonder in the presence of the Almighty and Transcendent God. This would be the way God would lead and teach me all my life. I would have an experience, later to be given the understanding. I found this very reassuring and reliable.

Attending a Catholic convent school up to the age of almost seventeen ensured at least a reasonable knowledge of the Faith, indeed Religious Education lessons in our final year at school were spent in teaching us how to defend our faith. Evidence of this ability comes to mind as I recall a particular occasion in the office.

I worked in an open office divided into two departments sharing the common space. There were ten of us in all and I was one of only four women, also the only Catholic. Usually the departments worked quietly, separately, and efficiently, each team engrossed in its various projects. Occasionally however, an extraordinarily sustained lull would descend.

It was usually Luigi who would break the silence with an imaginary roll of the drums, played out on the side of the metal filing cabinet, to attract everyone's attention. Once alerted, everyone would sit back in their chairs in anticipation.

Imitating a phrase remembered from the Latin Mass, "Dominus vobiscum" meaning, "The Lord be with you", Luigi would mockingly break into a chant of

"Who's for a game of dom..i..noes?"

Continuing in like manner, he would then reply to his own question with

"I..am!" drawled out, repeating the same tune of the first sentence.

We all knew the code. It was Luigi's way of suggesting an extra mid-morning or afternoon tea break. This little pantomime was funny to behold and even the departmental bosses joined in the 'game', which may then open up a discussion on a headline in the daily newspaper or some controversial issue of the day.

It was and could be taken in good sport, but occasionally it would take on a more contentious tone, opening up a serious question, often aimed at me against the Catholic Church.

Because of the silent suspense already created in the room, everyone was already sitting back in their seats to listen to Luigi trying to score points over me. I answered, confidently as far as I was able, and I hope respectfully, as we had been taught at school to respond in such a situation.

"Always be prepared to give an answer to everyone who asks you to give the reason for the hope that you have. But do this with gentleness and respect." (1 Peter 3:15)

After a period of questioning and answering subjects ranging from divorce, birth control, pre-marital sex and abortion, Luigi suddenly relented, acknowledging that, "not only can you answer the questions, but you can even anticipate them." Well done, St Joseph's! I quietly preened. Sister Monica would have been very pleased to hear such a statement.

Despite considerable knowledge, gained from learning about God, I could not yet claim to have a living relationship with Him. Even with those special numinous experiences, there was still something missing. I came to understand that part of the problem lay in the fact of having been merely educated in the faith, without the benefit of that all-important component, nurturing, bringing me back to the nature/ nurture debate once again. But at the end of the day, I now realise, God had His unique plans for my life and He knows when and how to reveal Himself to me.

"For I know the plans I have for you" declares the Lord, "plans to prosper you and not to harm you, plans to give you hope and a future." (Jeremiah 29:11)

CHANGES AFOOT
1957-1975

When I met my future husband, Tom, and his family, I felt, spiritually, rather like a struggling plant, which had suddenly been re-planted into rich soil. His family was devout and practised their faith. Despite her busy schedule, with five children and often lodgers from Ireland, Tom's mother, a fine Irish lady, went to Mass daily and faithfully led the family in night prayers. Their father, like my own, was a construction worker so was not usually in this little gathering, as he often worked away from home. As a regular Thursday night visitor, I joined the family in prayer and to this day, still say some of the prayers learned in those gatherings. So it was that, very gently, I began to receive something of the nurturing I had so longed to receive, as a plant naturally takes up its nourishment through osmosis.

After a courtship of four and a half years, Tom and I married in 1961 and I had every expectation that our marriage would move along without any complications. We thought we had prepared well for marriage, by attending Marriage Preparation classes, which called us to consider significant issues which might crop up in the future but which we might not necessarily have thought about yet.

We had not thought of how we might resolve serious differences between us or who was to take care of the family budget. Whether or not there was to be a 'Head' of the family or how we might consider ourselves equal were questions that made us pause and think. The classes also helped us to confirm our beliefs about the indissolubility of marriage. They also asked us both if we were aware of and comfortable with the Church's teaching on birth control.

Pauline 1959

It had been a very constructive exercise to consider these thought-provoking issues, but the questions I had were often of a quite different kind. I had an emptiness within, which no amount of external observances could satisfy. This was especially obvious when we went to Mass together. Tom seemed totally engrossed in the proceedings, and to see his devotion as he prayed was most humbling. It became obvious that his years of serving on the altar in his youth, plus the nurturing of his faith at home had deepened it to a level I could not even aspire to! In comparison to Tom, I felt much less involved, and to some degree still felt an outsider somehow, still pondering some aspects of our beliefs, which I dare not even admit to myself, let alone Tom! One subject which often came to mind, was why was I not 'on fire' as the

Apostles were after receiving the Holy Spirit at Pentecost? Nobody seemed to be answering that question nor, to my knowledge, even asking the question!

I do not wish to imply here that Tom's faith was in any way superficial, far from it, but he seemed totally content with the faith he had received and found it difficult to comprehend my questioning and searching. And when I briefly invited the Jehovah Witnesses in to do bible study, Tom gave me an ultimatum that I must not engage with them in any way.

It had all begun very innocently with that knock on the door, usually around the times of the great Christian feasts of Christmas and Easter, when the Witnesses, usually in twos, challenge the unsuspecting householder, on the doorstep, with their interpretations of certain Scriptures. I had fallen for this, and it was their challenging questions which first started me to search for answers in a Catholic version of the bible, which in turn set me on a lifelong bible reading venture. So, in spite of everything, I am grateful for that fateful knock on the door.

What Tom failed to understand, and I certainly could not have articulated it at the time, was that he had absorbed the Faith as naturally as through his mother's milk so to speak and learned to pray at his mother's knee. As a result, he felt secure in the Faith passed on to him and did not feel the need to question anything. Without the benefit of these advantages myself, I still had many questions. I was on a quest to find my own adult faith, whatever it took, and whatever the cost. It was a painful time as I struggled between faith and doubt, a spiritual 'rite of passage' as I moved from a child-like faith to a more mature and considered one, from which process I learned how to nurture myself, through a combination of prayer, study, and fellowship.

We married in 1961, just a year before the Second Vatican Council was convened. (This was a meeting of all the Catholic bishops of the world, summoned to consider how to make the Church more relevant in the then ever-changing world of the 1960s). The Council, consisting of some two thousand bishops, met from 1962 and concluded in 1965, during which time we heard snatches of new teachings and that significant changes to the practice of the Faith were afoot, as new theologies came into prominence. These were busy, life-changing years, for society, the Church and for us as a couple, for we were now proud parents of our first two beautiful children, Stephen and Anne, born in 1962 and 1963, respectively.

There were many changes to accommodate in the Church after the Council, disturbing to some and encouraging to others. What would appear trivial changes to some would appear catastrophic to others. One very significant change was in changing the language of the Mass from Latin to English (not universally but for English speaking countries). Other countries would similarly translate the Latin Mass into their own native language.

Speaking as one who had only rarely frequented a Latin Mass, this was joy to my ears – an opportunity to gain a better understanding of the sacred liturgy (Mass) now more clearly understood in my own language.

For the traditionalist, this was as good as a betrayal. Latin was our universal faith language and had been so since the Church's inception. On the other hand, the Mass in Latin came into being precisely because it was the common language spoken by most people - the 'lingua franca' of its day.

Pauline and Tom 1961.

How were we to bring these strongly opposing views together? Conversations about the subject could be heard breaking out whenever church people met.

Another issue, which might be considered a trivial one, was in the directive to remove altar rails. This seemed absolutely unthinkable and almost sacrilegious when viewed from one perspective, but thoroughly acceptable when viewed from another. It was all a question of equally valid but differing theologies, which were not being explained to the faithful at the time. Hence the turmoil.

Another important teaching emanating from the Council was that there is no such thing as a second-class Christian, in other words there is no hierarchical status to holiness. We are all holy by virtue of being joined to Christ in our Baptism. This teaching was one of many which were greatly misunderstood, causing many nuns and priests to leave the church.

Running through all the pastoral letters from that time to the present is the strong theme that everyone in the church is called to be a 'missionary.' It was probably this insight that revived my childhood memory with its limited understanding of being a missionary, and which now began to beg for my attention.

Because there was so much to absorb after the Council, I took advantage of any and all opportunities to learn about the new changes, especially taking very much to heart the words we heard in the Baptismal service, "You are your children's first teachers. May you be the best of teachers." To be this, I needed to gain as much knowledge as possible. I rejoiced at this opportunity to start afresh, to give to our children something of the nurturing I had not received myself.

But where was Tom in all the turmoil of those days? In today's parlance we would say, "Not a happy bunny." As a result, what had initially been a quest on my part to catch up with Tom's faith, had now caused us to start to walk on parallel paths! This was certainly something we could never have anticipated when we prepared for marriage. There were other issues too, which became apparent as time wore on.

One striking change after the Council was a refreshing openness to dialogue with other Christian faiths. After five centuries of separation following the Reformation, this goodwill on all sides freed me to accept the kind invitation of our neighbours, Joyce and Laurie, to join their prayer group from time to time. They were my first introduction to the Methodist church, and I liked what I saw.

My closest friend in those years was Mary, whom I met

at the school gates one day waiting for our children. We struck up an instant friendship and had much in common. She had a lively mind and proved to be someone with whom I could discuss all matters of concern and we spent many an hour discussing matters of faith, especially the changes that the Council had proposed.

We were a perfect match for one another, as our husbands were often not around much because of the nature of their work. Having served five years in the RAF, Tom was currently working as a Ground Engineer at Manchester airport, at the same time as studying at college in the evening to gain qualifications to become a Flight Engineer.

Mary's husband, Cliff, a Probation Officer, worked very long hours, often well into the evening, besides which he was one of the first students studying for a degree with the newly established Open University. Often, he would have to stay up until the early hours of the morning to follow his lectures on TV. Meanwhile, Mary was a friend with whom I could have in-depth discussions, especially about our common faith and we even managed to attend an occasional course together.

Tom eventually realised his dream to fly and was offered a chance to become a Flight Engineer, which inevitably necessitated having to move south to take up the position with BOAC. It was a great sadness to lose Mary's day-to-day friendship when we eventually moved in 1975, but we remained friends, though from a distance.

Another influential person of faith who came into my life in my early marriage was Mrs Rogers, a dear old lady who lived down the road and who needed help with her cleaning. As soon as I heard of this, I introduced myself and gladly helped her each Friday evening. Our friendship soon developed into something like a mother/daughter relationship and was mutually enriching, as she shared family stories with me. But, best of all, was the spiritual nourishment she unconsciously gave in sharing her deep Catholic Faith, reminding me of Psalm 1.

Such a one is like a tree planted near streams,
it bears fruit in season and its leaves never wither.
(NJ Psalm 1:3)

Until the day she died, her leaves never did fade! She was a worthy role model and mentor, one of those special Person Gifts which the Lord has given me along my (sometimes) lonely but richly blessed journey.

Sad as it was to leave our home in Hazel Grove, and family in the north, it was all in God's providence that we should move south, because there I would meet the next significant people along my faith journey.

Soon, new doors would open, new faith friends of influence would come into my life, and I would have an experience of the Holy Spirit, which I could not have anticipated nor imagined in a lifetime.

You shall seek Me and find Me when you seek Me
with all your heart (Jeremiah 29:13)

BLESSED ARE THOSE
WHO MOURN
July 1970

Several months had passed since the death of my mother, and my thoughts were presently preoccupied by my pending operation for varicose veins. With hospital bag packed for my brief stay of five days, I searched around for something to read during the long and tedious hours on the ward. Just the thing, I thought, when I spied a copy of *Readers' Digest* recently passed to me.

Having unpacked my belongings into the locker at my bedside, I set myself into a comfortable reading position on top of the bed and looked at the index of titles. One caught my attention immediately because it intrigued me. It concerned a group of scientists who were investigating people's preternatural or supernatural accounts.

Sometime later, the patient in the neighbouring bed called out, "You've not had your head out of that book since you arrived; it must be interesting." She followed this with a quizzical expression, which seemed to indicate her query warranted an explanation, or at least a response.

What had begun as merely an opening to a conversation between two strangers, quickly developed into an amazing revelation and supernatural experience in my own life. My fellow patient went on to explain that she had a special gift, sometimes, of knowing something about a person, which she could not possibly have known by normal means. This unnerved me somewhat, as I felt the conversation steering towards what sounded to me like Spiritualism, the practice of trying to communicate with the spirits of the dead, especially through mediums, which, my Catholic faith taught, should be avoided.

"But I don't pursue this," she said, "and besides which, I, too, am a Catholic and know the Church's teaching on these things." With this retort, by way of explanation, we moved onto other topics in our lives.

The next few days flew by in a series of pre- and post-operative procedures. It was now day five and we were waiting to be transported home, when my newfound friend opened up with a surprise statement. "Do you remember our first conversation?" How could I forget it! It had been well beyond my comprehension and former experience.

"Well, I have had a revelation concerning you. It was the night the older gentleman visited you. Was that your father?" With my quick affirmative, she continued. "During that visit I had a vision of a woman. She didn't speak but she was looking so lovingly at both of you, and the overriding impression was that you were not to worry as she was at peace." As she described the vision, her description of the woman was strikingly like my mother, especially when she made the odd remark that the vision of the woman showed only to the woman's knees. The lower legs were not visible.

This description seemed to point all the more to the likelihood that it was my mother she had seen, because in later life she was unable to walk, as a result of rheumatoid arthritis in her knees. Her lower limbs were useless.

Then she directed another question to me. "Was your mother very fond of your children? I ask this because she was cradling a baby in her arms and, from time to time, was affectionately drawing the infant's face close to hers as she gently kissed it." I did not need to think long to answer this, save for one thing. I had three children and she loved all of them equally.

Just then, time did not allow for any further discussion because our various modes of transport were awaiting us.

What was I to make of this experience? Could I share it with my father, or would it be too insensitive so soon after my mother's death? I needed to ponder a little more and pray for wisdom.

To understand the implications of this revelation, I need to share something of mine and my father's grieving process since the loss of my mother. Mum had died in February; it was now July and every day since her death, my father had somehow felt compelled to visit her grave, walking a round trip of six to seven miles, feeling unable to let her go.

He had nursed her at home for many months and only the day before her death, she had asked the doctor to place her in hospital. Letting her slip from his care felt like a betrayal of sorts.

I had been sworn to secrecy about the seriousness of her condition, but I guess she had become aware herself that the end was near and preferred to avoid further distress for my father and brother by staying at home.

I did eventually recount the episode to my father. Not only did he accept the story, but he had already started to feel free of the burden of guilt that he might have been able to do more for her. Soon, the daily visits to the grave were spaced out and his life began to take on a more normal pace and routine.

My grieving process was quite different. At the news of my mother's impending death, I made an appointment to see the family doctor for his prognosis. Yes, her condition was terminal but, he emphasised, "You mustn't tell her so. She is a fighter and will do her utmost to fight it. On the other hand, if you tell her the truth, she will 'put her face to the wall' and give up." My father said much the same and swore me to secrecy. Thus, I was obliged to respect their wishes.

For me, this posed a tremendous problem. Knowing my mother to be a woman for whom truth was paramount, I found this approach bewildering. Besides, I felt the priest should be informed, to prepare her spiritually, and to be ready to administer the Last Rites when the time came.

For nine long weeks we played this game of subterfuge, until one day my father appeared at my front door to inform me that Mum had asked to go into hospital. With this news, I arranged to visit with my brother in the evening, which is where this story picks up.

We found Mum in a confused state of mind, on the one hand requesting something of us, only to find in the next moment that that was not what she had intended. She remained in this very muddled state for most of the visit.

We were just coming to the end of the prescribed visiting hour when she called for a drink. Springing immediately to meet her request, I searched in the surrounding rooms for a kitchen where I might get the drink. Unfortunately, the rooms were being used for other purposes and I had to return to her bedside, mission unfulfilled, with not a nurse in sight to pass on her request.

My brother called for us to leave, as the final bell for end of visiting had already sounded, adding, reassuringly, "The nurses will soon be round with the night-time drink, and they will see to her." With that, we left the ward and made our way home. That was the last time I saw her, and to think I had not met her last request!

Early the next morning the message from the hospital came, for my father to go there immediately. Poor Dad, he could not face the end alone, and instead of going straight to the hospital, waited for me to accompany him.

By the time we arrived, Mum had already died. The ward Sister was furious that my dad had not gone straight to the hospital and no attempt on my part to explain the reason softened her. "But," she added, impatiently, "at least the priest was with her at the end." This extremely hurtful remark wounded deeply, but despite this, what a comfort to know that my prayers were answered, by the completely unexpected way in which Mum had received the final comfort of the Last Rites.

Nevertheless, I still carried the lingering guilt of not

meeting her last request, which haunted me constantly, UNTIL that revelation from my fellow patient, that all was well with my mother, and that Dad and I should be at peace, because she was.

There is one final thing to add to this story. My first interpretation of the vision was that perhaps the baby in my mother's arms was her first child, who had been stillborn. About three months after the vision, however, I became pregnant with our fourth child, but sadly I miscarried. Was this the baby in the vision? Was I not only being comforted about my mother's death but also receiving a foretelling of another grandchild's death and a promise that Mum would take care of it? Whatever the reality is, I took great comfort from this chance meeting in hospital and thank God for it.

Blessed are those who mourn,
for they shall be comforted (Matthew 5:4)

FROM MOTHER TO
BROWN OWL
1975

We had not intended to live in Yateley, Hampshire, and indeed we had our name on a new house to be built just over the county border in Frimley Green, Surrey, however, when we came to register the children in the schools we had chosen, we found to our dismay that the house was not in the catchment area. It was August 1975, and the new school year was rapidly approaching, so it was with some degree of panic that we contacted the local estate agents to see if they had any properties suitable to our needs. Luckily, a suitable property was identified in the then small village of Yateley.

We checked out the house, considering it at the time as merely a stopgap home to move into until we had time to familiarise ourselves with what the area had to offer. I am now writing this forty-five years later and I am still in that 'stopgap' house! So, what has caused us to stay here?

Having checked out the house we decided to have a look at our soon-to-be parish church, St Swithun's. As soon as we entered the building, I fell in love with the architecture of the church. Its octagonal design, slightly sloping floor leading down to the sanctuary, plus the openness of the pews, positioned to allow the parishioners to see across the aisles, gave the congregation a sense of togetherness. A later parish priest from Nigeria, Father Dominic Adeiza shared his first impressions of the Church. He first saw an aerial view of it and pointed out the unusual octagonal roof shape, which reminded him of a crown. Thereafter, whenever he referred to the parish, he called us, 'The Royal Parish', which we all delighted in.

After moving into the house and our new parish, we were surprised at the few numbers of parishioners who attended Mass each Sunday, in contrast to the very different scenario in the north, where it was necessary to arrive at Church very early in order to be accommodated inside. Many a time, we had to stand outside and listen to Mass being celebrated but, of course, we had not appreciated that there are many more Catholics in the north of England.

Soon after we moved into Yateley, Tom was offered a six-month secondment with Gulf Air (who had bought British Airways VC10s and needed crews to fly them), during which time the children and I settled into our new environment. I soon became involved in various aspects of parish life. For example, I enquired from our parish priest, Father Carroll, what opportunities there were for young teenagers (Stephen was shortly to turn fourteen and Anne was close behind). Without a moment's hesitation, Father Carroll said, "Nothing, so what are you going to do about it?" Before waiting for an answer, he walked over to the filing cabinet and selected six or seven names of young people of similar age and with these gave me the name of a young man, Mike who was also interested in setting something up for the youth. Thus, 'The Parish Youth Group' was formed.

I like to say, when telling of its origins, 'I went to the meeting merely as a concerned mother. I came back a somewhat unofficial Brown Owl.'

The group took the form of a discussion and social group, meeting alternatively in mine and Mike's house but we also undertook other activities, such as camping and sponsored walks. The group held together until they moved on in their studies, either at College or University. Many still have contact with each other to this day even though many miles separate some of them.

RICKY
1976

They say never volunteer, don't they? On this occasion, I was responding to a request to join The Liturgy Committee. I did not exactly know what they were about, but I would quickly learn, so I supposed.

So, with an open mind I went to my first meeting with the group and my breath was taken away with what I experienced. One member of the small committee was an American Airman based near Newbury but living in Yateley.

The work of the meeting began quietly enough, preparing for any significant feasts in the liturgical calendar in the months ahead. When it was Ricky's turn to speak, he became extremely animated about an experience he had had and was desperate to share it with us. He started by bringing out a copy of the Bible, and pointing to it, saying that ever since he had experienced the 'Baptism in the Holy Spirit,' (an expression none of us was familiar with), he felt compelled to read the Bible. It was as if it were 'speaking' to him, and the words were personally addressed to him. Since his experience, he was reading it every night into the early hours of the morning, His passion was infectious, at least to me. Not so to the rest of the group who were anxious to get on with the 'real' business of the meeting.

I did not actually understand what Ricky was talking about because it was quite out of my frame of reference, but I knew one thing - I wanted what he had! Hadn't I been praying for this very same thing for twenty years? I used to say to myself, "I believe all that I have been taught about Jesus, but why am I not 'on fire' as the Apostles were at Pentecost?" This had been my one desire for all that time. Now I was meeting someone who was alive with the Holy Spirit. I do not remember anything that was discussed that night, but I longed to get to know Ricky and looked forward to meeting him at the next Liturgy Meeting.

I rushed home that evening, eager to share with Tom, about this amazing encounter with what I described as "a real Christian." This turn of phrase did not sit well with Tom, but I knew intuitively that what I had seen in Ricky was authentic.

I shall always be grateful for that chance meeting at the Liturgy Group. Ricky was certainly an inspiration and a catalyst for my own personal renewal. Meanwhile, I would just keep on with my quest, until another Ricky appeared so I could take the next step.

"When the student is ready, the teacher appears; and when the student is truly ready, the teacher disappears"
(often attributed to Toa Te Ching)

BAPTISM IN THE HOLY SPIRIT
c. 1978

Time passed since meeting Ricky at the Liturgy meeting and I wondered why I never saw him at Mass, but I later learned he had been repatriated to the States after completing his service in England. I also learned he had left the Catholic Church, having become despondent at the lack of affirmation, understanding, or even support as he struggled to process and articulate his incredible encounter with the Holy Spirit, for which he had no adequate vocabulary. On his return to the States, he had found a temporary spiritual 'home' within the Pentecostal church.

It would have been beyond my wildest dreams at that moment to even consider that I too would be privileged to experience, a year or so later, what Ricky had falteringly referred to as 'Renewal', later known as 'Baptism in the Holy Spirit.' Regrettably, I too suffered the same negative reaction from most people whenever I spoke enthusiastically about my experience of the Holy Spirit.

I can see now, in retrospect, several distinct stages in which the Holy Spirit was directing my life, through certain individuals and, interestingly, three convents, which were to be significant places in those stages.

Stage 1. Yateley Convent

My first encounter with the 'Renewal' or the 'Charismatic' Movement as it was later called, was when the parish invited the Wokingham Prayer Group to lead an evening of Prayer and Praise. Little did I imagine that I would be the only person from the parish to respond to the invitation. Looking back on this history some forty-plus years later, it seems almost to have been like a personal invitation.

The evening took place in Yateley Convent, located in the church grounds. Truth to tell, I did not quite know what to make of it all. They sang, with great passion and feeling, beautiful hymns I had never heard before and I witnessed spontaneous prayer for the first time. Even more remarkable was when the group suddenly erupted into spontaneous singing, which I later learned was 'Singing in the Spirit' or 'Singing in Tongues.' Each person appeared to be singing in a different language, with their own unique melody, yet beautifully intertwining with each other. Instead of producing what might have been a cacophony of sounds, they blended harmoniously. Even more startling to the hearer was the way in which the singing finally came to a close, as if an invisible conductor were conducting!

Stranger still was when one of the group prayed alone in an unknown language. This was followed by a pause while the group, it seemed to me, held its breath as if waiting for something, which eventually occurred when another member broke the silence speaking, this time in English, and gave an 'interpretation' of the prophetic message given earlier in Tongues. What I had been witnessing for the first time in my life was a manifestation of some of the Gifts of the Spirit mentioned in 1 Corinthians 12 and elsewhere in the Scriptures.

Despite this incredible introduction to Gifts of the Holy Spirit, nonetheless because of its strangeness and unfamiliarity, which had taken me quite out of my comfort zone, I decided it was not for me. Thankfully, the Lord had other plans, which was how I met Peter Carty, who was the parishioner who had initiated the invitation of the Wokingham Prayer Group to Yateley.

After the meeting, Peter made enquiries to find out who I was and where I lived. One day, he turned up at my door, asking what I thought of the meeting. Despite my gentle protestations of "nice but not for me," he almost pleaded with me to attend a 'Day of Renewal' held monthly in Alton Convent, so I could give 'The Renewal' another try, once more in the 'safe' environment of a convent where, I was assured, some of the nuns attended.

Stage 2. Alton Convent
After much persuasion, I agreed to attend the next Day of Renewal. This was in the late 1970s when Renewal was young in England, having swept over from America, where this new 'Move' of the Holy Spirit with its renewal of the Gifts of the Spirit had started. Although I did not know it then, Alton Convent was to play a huge part in my eventual

'Baptism in the Holy Spirit,' but before that I need to tell you about my first visit.

Peter had warned that we had to arrive early because these gatherings were growing in popularity, with people driving for miles to attend. Despite arriving in good time, we found ourselves unable to get into the chapel, which was originally built to accommodate about one hundred people, now bulging at the seams with maybe more than two hundred! As a result, we were jammed in the foyer, however we could hear everything and, being tall, I could see most of the proceedings.

The format for the day was a half hour of Prayer and Praise, followed by a talk from an invited guest, shared afternoon tea and finally closing with Mass.

As soon as the Prayer and Praise began, I was immediately transported to the evening in Yateley Convent and began to sense the same joy in the people, which was tangible. When people spoke out loud in spontaneous prayer, there was no embarrassment or discomfort in talking to God in an intimate, informal way. Instead, they spoke lovingly and freely to God. I was extremely impressed with the deep reverence with which they addressed God. Soon, I became aware of a sentence forming in my mind:

"Take off your sandals, for the place where you are standing is holy ground" (Exodus 3:5)

Even within my limited knowledge of the Bible at that time, I readily recognised the words spoken to Moses at the burning bush, when he found himself in the Presence of God.

Yes, I thought to myself, I'm on Holy Ground, and what is more, these people are holy, too. I was in the very 'Presence' of God! If space had allowed me to kneel, I would have done so. Instead, I 'knelt with my heart,' never to be quite the same again. Was this what Ricky had been trying to convey in that fateful Liturgy meeting?

After this moving experience, I began to attend the Day of Renewal each month. At first, a strange phenomenon occurred. I enjoyed the Prayer and Praise and joined in with gusto as I learned the new hymns (songs we called them), which gave a more intimate feel to the worship. When the time for the invited speaker arrived to address the meeting however, a strange heaviness enveloped me, and I was unable to keep awake! It was very embarrassing, but hard as I tried, I could not stay awake for the message! I came to the conclusion that, for whatever reason, I was not ready to receive it. How true that was, as my next encounter with the Holy Spirit proved.

Stage 3. Farnborough Hill Convent
A Day's Retreat at Farnborough Hill Convent proved to be another significant steppingstone towards my 'Baptism in the Holy Spirit' though I had no idea it would play such a significant part in my conversion.

The speaker for the day was Rev. Deacon Pat Taylor from Basingstoke. I cannot remember what he spoke about that day, but I know he impressed me enough to seek him out at the end of the day and to confide in him what was troubling me spiritually. He listened kindly and intently, finally writing down his name and telephone number on the only available bit of paper we could find - a cigarette packet, promising to pray for me. In the meantime, I was free to take him up on his offer to contact him to discuss further what was on my mind.

For the moment it was sufficient to know that someone now knew of my intense inner sadness and was praying for me. Although our discussion was not sacramental Confession, I felt unburdened to a degree. At that moment, it was enough to know that he was praying for me. Things might have ended there, but unknown to me, I was still a work in progress as far as the Holy Spirit was concerned.

Alton Day of Renewal – Vision of a Festering Wound
On the third or fourth Day of Renewal which I attended at Alton, I found myself earnestly praying to God to change my heart and to forgive me for my lack of forgiveness towards a family member who had wounded me deeply with their hurtful words. As I prayed, asking for forgiveness, and telling God I hated the bitter resentful person I was rapidly becoming, I became deeply disturbed by the frightening picture forming in my mind, of a deep, fleshy, festering wound.

My eyes jerked open immediately as I wondered why such an image should come to me. Closing my eyes once more to continue the prayer, again the same picture presented itself, with the same response from me. When the vision occurred a third time, I resisted opening my eyes to avoid seeing the dreadful sight yet knowing instinctively I was meant to watch it. I had to 'face' it so to speak, to acknowledge my sin. My heart flooded with repentance, as I took in what I was being forced to acknowledge. This image was the state of my soul!

The moment I repented, the vision changed dramatically. No longer was it a deep, fleshy septic wound but was, at once, completely clean. The wound was still deep, but no longer filled with the poisonous bitterness, which my lack of forgiveness had caused. Now, it was completely clean.

Once I comprehended what the image represented, it began to change again as I watched. It was as if an invisible seamstress were, in one corner, starting to close up the once gaping mouth of the wound. After only a few invisible stitches, the vision abruptly ended.

They say a picture paints a thousand words; my vision certainly did so. The Psalmist has it succinctly:

My guilt has overwhelmed me like a burden too heavy to bear. My wounds fester and are loathsome because of my sinful folly... I confess my iniquity, I am troubled by my sin. (Psalm 38:4, 5, 18)

Given time to reflect on this aspect of the vision, I came to understand that the closing of the wound represented healing. What I had been shown was the state of my soul before and after repentance. Repentance had removed the sin of un-forgiveness, leaving the wound (my soul) cleansed of sin. Healing was then possible, but healing, I learned, is a process not an event, thus my healing would be ongoing and that would still require my future co-operation and ongoing conversion.

I had been suffering with severe back pain for seven years before this event, which doctors had diagnosed as psychosomatic (disharmony between body and soul), but within a few days of confessing my sin, the pain had gone. This was replaced by an immense inner joy and sense of the Holy Spirit 'singing' within me. I was not able to realise quite what this meant, until I later read from Scripture the following verse:

"I will repay you for the years the locusts have eaten"
(Joel 2:25)

I began to realise the truth of this verse, as the sensation of the Holy Spirit singing in my heart lasted for exactly the same length of time as I had held onto my resentment. Now, the sadness of those years had been replaced by joy and inner contentment.

Alton Day of Renewal – The Grace of Baptism in the Holy Spirit

At the next Day of Renewal which I attended, something remarkable happened. Not only was I able to stay awake for the talk, but I now listened intently. My spiritual ears had been opened to spiritual things, and I had even purchased for myself, in the meantime, a small pocket-size edition of the New Testament and was delving into it during my lunch breaks at work.

The Alton Day of Renewal became my place of renewal,

refreshment and, most importantly, fellowship (a very New Testament word, which I came to love and treasure for all that it meant in my newfound experience with people of like-mind who, too, had been touched by the Spirit). The best way to describe how I felt was that my heart was singing and Scripture seemed as if it were speaking directly to me. A new vocabulary was beginning to form when thinking or speaking of God. Scripture became increasingly more significant and seemed to be addressing me personally for the first time in my life.

No Day of Renewal at Alton could ever be described as 'ordinary' or 'usual.' They were all special, sanctified by the Presence of the Holy Spirit. That said, all my experiences so far could not compare with what was to happen on one particular Day of Renewal.

I wasn't aware of the name of the speaker before going that day but was thrilled when it turned out to be Deacon Pat Taylor. I thought to myself, I might have known he would be a part of the Renewal, for he had a special glow about him and, I later learned, he had the Gift of Healing.

Later, as the group started to make its way to the hall for a shared tea, I had to pass Deacon Pat, who was standing at the door acknowledging people. As I approached, I did not expect him to remember me, so I reminded him of how and where we had met before. Yes, he did remember me and had prayed every day since for my intention. Gently, he probed how 'things' were, to which I replied, "The situation hasn't changed, but I have changed," thinking of the vision of the wound and my repentant response.

To my surprise, Pat then asked something which took me aback somewhat. Could he pray with me? It was just the unfamiliar preposition he used which caught my attention. Usually, we would use pray for whoever/whatever. Feeling somewhat embarrassed and a little guilty at taking up his time, I answered somewhat inanely, "Yes, if you've got the time." Pointing towards the altar steps, Pat asked if I would meet him there after the flow of people had subsided. Accordingly, I made my way to the appointed place waiting nervously, joined by my friend Gladys. Within minutes, Pat joined us and quickly began to pray 'over' me, with arms outstretched, finally laying both hands upon my head while he called upon the Holy Spirit. I had not been prayed with like that since my Confirmation when the bishop laid his hands in like manner.

Words fail me to explain what happened next, but when I recovered from the experience, I was lying on the floor. (The Holy Spirit sometimes causes a person to fall as if in a faint). I did not know about this phenomenon at the time, which convinces me of the authenticity of my experience even more. American Pentecostals had the expression, being 'slain' in the Spirit. We English, with our reserve, had refined this to 'resting in the Spirit.' Whatever the term, as Pat and Gladys helped me from the ground, I do remember asking, "What on earth has just happened to me?" "You've just received a tremendous outpouring of the Holy Spirit." With that, Pat excused himself to join the other people in the hall, but asked me to stay awhile, to thank God for such a wonderful blessing.

Before I could formulate words to thank God, a sensation from the depths of my being began to flood my whole body from my feet upwards. As the sensation filled more and more of my body, I realised I could name it. It was pure JOY and as it moved upwards towards my mouth, I felt I could not contain such joy, so with hand over mouth, I quickly made my way to a side exit. It would be so inappropriate, I thought, to laugh out loud in church, but once outside, I exploded into unspeakably joyous laughter!

I clearly remember Gladys' face. One minute she had seen me lying prostrate on the floor, as I received the Baptism in the Holy Spirit. Now I was laughing as though drunk! But this was a second Pentecost! All this made sense when I looked at the story of the first Pentecost. In that account, in Acts, Chapter 2, the people of Jerusalem who heard the Apostles thought they, too, were drunk, but as St Peter pointed out, they were not drunk with wine but on the Holy Spirit. Besides, it was only nine o'clock in the morning.

Before setting off for home, I waited for this incredible joy to abate somewhat, which was like waiting for the bubbles in a glass of champagne to subside. Nevertheless, we had an interesting incident on our return journey. Following Gladys' directions, I accidentally drove down a one-way street the wrong way. Quickly realising my mistake, I made a hurried right turn, drove around the block, bringing me out facing the right way. We had, however, been spotted by a policeman, who saw my quick manoeuvre and was there waiting, having already booked us!

I was horrified and most apologetic. The officer looked us

over, ignoring Gladys' protestations that she was to blame because she had directed me. Something softened the police officer's heart (was it the Holy Spirit?) and he finished by apologising to us for having so rashly booked us when he saw our manoeuvre! We will never know why we were not formally charged that day but one friend, hearing this story said, "You were not booked because you had the 'Ring of Confidence' around you!" I've never heard the Holy Spirit called that before!

My new 'Life in the Spirit' had just begun.

ON EAGLES' WINGS
1979

The first stage of this family holiday was in the fabulous Seychelles. Here, Tom was delighted to show us his favourite destination of all and to share with us some of the privileges he had in flying with British Airways.

I remember distinctly being stunned by the unspoiled natural beauty of the Seychelles, in stark contrast with Bermuda with its manicured lawns and golf courses. Unlike the turquoise waters of Bermuda, the sea here was a beautiful royal blue colour in the deeper parts, with various shades of blue depending on the depths of the water.

Our means of travel around Mahe, the main island, was by means of a mini-moke - a small jeep, which we all managed to scramble into, with the kids taking turns to change sides to avoid being burned by the bright sun. Tourists in numbers had not yet discovered this tropical paradise, aptly named 'The Garden of Eden,' so after visiting the capital, Victoria, most of our time was spent travelling around from place to place and inevitably ending up on the beach. It was here that the kids were first introduced to paragliding, which was quite hair-raising to watch, but fortunately they were carefully supervised by Tom and in case of problems, such as ditching in the shallow water, all three were competent swimmers.

Meanwhile, having settled myself beneath a coconut palm for shade, I started to read a book. The peace, however, was soon disturbed by the frantic shouting of one of the hotel waiters who was gesturing to me to move away from the tree. Apparently, one of the coconuts was about to fall, very likely on top of my head! He came over to explain his concern. A lady had been hurt badly just the day before by a coconut falling from that very tree. With this information, I had the option of moving into the sun and getting sunburnt or risk injury from a falling coconut!

Having moved to what I considered a safer spot, I returned once again to the book, *My Father is the Gardener* by Colin Urquhart, which was his account of experiencing the Baptism in the Holy Spirit, as I had done myself only a few months earlier.

The author was writing about his changed life since his experience of the Holy Spirit but which he, frustratedly, could not convey adequately to his wife. I empathised with this dilemma, since I, too, could not convey to Tom or indeed to any of my friends what I, also, had experienced. A couple of years later, I would read his wife's own testimony and took consolation and encouragement that one day I, too, might be able to share freely with Tom what I was now experiencing. That day would come eventually, 'in God's good time' as they say.

Despite being in possibly the most beautiful place in the

world, my attention was not on the natural beauty around me but, instead, I was riveted to the pages of the book. I had never read or heard anyone speak of the Holy Spirit as this author did. Fully engrossed in the book, I thus spent the final couple of days of our holiday in the Seychelles.

We had made a decision a few days earlier to break our holiday to make a stopover in Bahrain to visit old friends we had known when we lived in the north of England. We were able to do this at short notice because we were travelling on an open ticket, which gave us more flexibility to make slight changes, such as date changes, however, we could not use other carriers.

Those were the days before we had credit cards, so expenses had to be very carefully calculated and relevant currency arranged before departure. Since it was an afterthought to visit Bahrain, we had not considered that our Seychelles money would not be acceptable there. However, our friends, Pete and Eileen, covered our expenses for the couple of days we were there, until such time as we could arrange to repay them.

After a very pleasant stay with them, we made our way to the airport to catch the once-a-day flight back to the UK. We had seriously misjudged our chances of securing five seats for the family and were requested by the airport staff to try again the following night (around midnight). By the time we arrived back at our friends' house, it was about one a.m. and we had to wake them up to stay for another night. It was embarrassing for us, but Pete and Eileen were very gracious about it.

The following night, we went through the same procedure, only to experience the same outcome. We felt like the proverbial bad pennies rolling back a second time. This was truly, truly embarrassing but we had no alternative but to wake up the household once again.

A third night came, and we hit the same problem, not sufficient seats available on the flight to London. Just when we were wondering what we should do next, and dreading the thought of disturbing our hosts yet again, son, Peter whispered into my ear, "Have you asked God to help us, Mum?" The question shamed me. Here I was reading about all the marvellous things God had done in the life of Colin Urquhart, yet it had not occurred to me that He could or would intervene in our situation. Prompted by Peter's suggestion, and encouraged by a sudden inner conviction, I sent up a prayer calling on God to help us, now with the confident assurance and expectation that God would help us. (I later heard this described by a priest as an infused 'Gift of Faith' mentioned in the list of Charismatic Gifts outlined in 1 Corinthians, Chapter 12).

Hardly five minutes went by after the prayer was uttered when we were approached by the Airport Superintendent. The ground staff had pointed out our family to him, explaining that this was our third attempt to leave, and he took pity on us and promised to see what he could do about our plight. He knew that a flight from Sydney was due in for a refuelling stop in an hour, but he doubted whether it would have five empty seats.

Minutes later, he came back with the astonishing news

that there were exactly five empty seats, though scattered around the cabin. And, he had even managed to change our ticket to allow for the change of airline. Hardly had the wave of relief rippled over us at the news, when he shocked us by announcing that the flight was not actually going to the UK! Its destination was Frankfurt, but he assured us that once in Europe we would quickly get a flight back to the UK.

The flight to Frankfurt was comfortable. No sooner had we arrived at Frankfurt and put our names down for the next London flight when our names were called, and we were invited to board the London flight. After some of the long-haul flights we had become accustomed to, this part of our journey seemed merely a hop, skip and a jump.

On arrival at Heathrow and just when we were all breathing an enormous sigh of relief, there was another hitch. We watched the luggage carousel go round and round until all the luggage had been claimed, but there was no sign of ours! Enquiries were made and we learned that because we had such a rapid turnaround at Frankfurt, our luggage had not been transferred quickly enough from the Australian aircraft.

We had no idea how long our luggage would take to catch up with us, so rather than the whole family waiting around, getting hungrier by the minute, we drove home, with Tom gallantly volunteering to return for the luggage when it eventually arrived. Up to this point, I could see the Hand of God in helping us at each stage of the journey, so why this hitch? But barely had we arrived home when the telephone rang. It was the airport to inform us that the luggage had arrived and would be delivered to our door by taxi!

Whenever I recall this episode in our lives, I say to myself, as indeed I said to the family at the time, "When you are in God's Hands, He even carries your bags." From this episode, I learned that God works not only in the lives of people such as Colin Urquhart, but also in the lives of ordinary folks such as you and me. The following Scripture captures the essence of what we experienced.

"I carried you on eagles' wings" (Exodus19:4)

SEEK FIRST THE KINGDOM
OF GOD
July 1979

This reflection begins in the autumn of 1978 and our daughter, Anne's, choosing of 'O' levels for the following summer.

Passing through the dining room, where Anne and Tom were still sitting at the table after dinner, I caught a snatch of their conversation. "You'll have to ask your mother." I smiled to myself on hearing this expression, an oft used one by Tom, sometimes in jest. It could sound as if Tom were passing the buck to excuse himself from a parental commitment, but this was not the case. They had been discussing Anne's proposed choice of subjects for 'O' level the following summer. The problem was a clash with geography and history, both of which, unfortunately, fell in the same teaching period.

Anne, however, had found a solution; an Evening Class covering the same syllabus was being run at the local secondary school. Tom was agreeable to this in principle, but since his job took him away from home for a good deal of the time, the problem was the question of transporting Anne to and fro in the evenings. But, if I were agreeable, I could undertake this duty, hence the overheard familiar phrase. Needless to say, as most mums would, I was happy to oblige, indeed proud that Anne was showing such initiative.

By the time registration for the course arrived, I had decided to register myself also. I liked the syllabus, the Tudors and the Stuarts, and since I didn't have an 'O' level in history, I was quite keen to acquire another subject.

It was strange to be back in a school environment at first, but, with our excellent tutor, I found the new learning experience very stimulating. Week by week, I managed to keep up with homework assignments but struggled to do any additional reading due to the demands of an exacting full-time job and a family and household to run. Thus, as the examination time grew nearer, I was panicking somewhat.

The solution, I decided, was to take a week from my annual leave allowance to revise. With this arrangement carefully in place and my competitive spirit fully engaged, I was all set.

Unfortunately, on the day before my leave was to start, one of our neighbours came round, in a very anxious state. He was due to go on an overseas business trip, but his wife had become unwell. They had two small children at the time, both under school age. The neighbour wanted to know if I could watch over his wife and family in his absence.

My first thought, naturally, was about my study plan. "Of course," I found myself saying, supposing I could manage both commitments. Very quickly, though, I realised that his wife was much sicker than he had thought, so I arranged to take her to see her GP.

"Thank God, you've brought her," was his pronouncement. She was on the verge of a nervous breakdown and would need constant monitoring and care. With that prognosis, I had to abandon any thought of just popping round to check on the family. Now, I would have to devote all my time to looking after them. So it was that my study plan was thwarted, much to my dismay and disappointment.

Once I came to terms with the new situation and had put it into perspective, I comforted myself with the biblical exhortation:

"But seek first His kingdom and His Righteousness."
(Matthew 6:33)

Yes, to do the right thing in God's eyes was paramount, so I abandoned any thought of taking the examination.

A few days after the visit to the doctor, Tom surprised me one day when I popped home. He knew the degree of disappointment I was feeling at not being able to study, so he had recorded my notes onto tapes, so that I could listen to them during quiet periods, such as when the young children were asleep. How lucky to have such a kind and thoughtful husband!

"And all these things will be given to you as well."
(Matthew 6:33)

I relished every opportunity to listen to the tapes, and, in fact, as I was answering the exam questions a few weeks later, I could actually hear Tom's voice in my head!

Several weeks later, the exam results arrived, and, to my

astonishment, I had passed, and with an 'A' grade to boot! Thanks to Tom's loving gesture, God's promise had been fulfilled, proving once again that God does indeed move in mysterious ways, as the saying goes. Anne, too, was able to add history to her other nine 'O' levels!

THE PRAYER GROUP IS BORN
1980-1990

Attending Days of Renewal at Alton Convent each month became essential as a means of keeping in touch with the Renewal Movement and with new friends who, like me, had experienced the power and presence of the Holy Spirit. I had tried in vain to explain it to Father Carroll and others at church, eventually realising I was in the same position as Ricky had been at that first liturgy meeting.

It was as if a lifeline had been thrown out to me the day that I learned that Deacon Pat Taylor had a prayer meeting every Wednesday evening in Basingstoke, which I quickly joined, to supplement the monthly Day of Renewal.

In contrast to the exuberant praise of the Day of Renewal, in Pat's meetings, we learned to sit in silence and to wait on the Lord, rather like the practice of the Quakers. It was in such silences that I felt the physical presence of the Holy Spirit, in the form of a warm, gentle sensation cradling my face, as one does with a child to express one's love. Such moments confirmed to me just how much the Lord loves His children.

After a while, Christine, one of the mums whom I had

come to know through the school run, asked me outright one day, "What has happened to you? You look different, you're glowing!" Dare I try to tell her, and possibly suffer the same reaction of indifference or even outright ridicule? Something told me her question was genuine, so I gave a quick precis of my experience of Baptism in the Holy Spirit and subsequent weekly visits to Pat Taylor's group in Basingstoke. Obviously further intrigued, she wanted to know more. "Come and see," I said, echoing the words of Philip to Nathanael in the Gospel of John (John 1:46).

Christine took up my invitation and soon became a regular companion on Wednesday evenings. In turn, she gave the same invitation to her mother, Pat and her friends, Colette and Mary H. In like manner, Ros and Carol also joined us as the chain of invitation passed from one to another as each of them gave their testimony of how their lives were also being changed. So, little by little, we had become a sizeable group, filling three cars in convoy every week to attend the prayer meeting.

Week by week, Deacon Pat began to open the Scriptures to us and, in due course, we also started to attend the newly formed Basingstoke Day of Renewal, led by Deacon Pat and Sister Paddy from the Alton convent.

We might have continued indefinitely travelling to weekly prayer meetings in Basingstoke, had it not been for an invitation from the Wokingham prayer group for us to join them in an evening of prayer and praise to be held once again at Yateley Convent.

In the early days of Renewal, prayer meetings could

last until nearly midnight, which posed a problem for our hosts, the nuns. As ten o'clock came round on the evening of the return visit, we began to receive gentle signals from the nuns to bring a close to the evening, but for us the meeting was in full swing. At this point, Peter Carty, who had arranged the evening, asked if we could continue the meeting in my house because it was more suitable for the number of people than his own little cottage.

Soon, we had decamped and moved to my house, where we continued with prayer and praise 'till about 11.30 pm!

As the evening eventually came to its close, I was asked why it was that we travelled all the way to Basingstoke every Wednesday evening, a round trip of twenty-four miles, to attend a prayer meeting, when we could hold our own meetings in Yateley, more specifically, in my house!

"We haven't got a leader," I protested. Back came the swift reply, "Just meet together, in faith, and the Lord will indicate who is to lead, or send you a leader."

So it was that the Yateley Prayer Group was born, and, despite my protestations, the group decided I was to lead. My earlier experiences of working with the youth group and later as a catechist for Confirmation had given me some basic skills in facilitating a group, which stood me in good stead. Now, I was to learn a completely new skill, that of being sensitive to the promptings of the Holy Spirit within a group. I am so glad for the blessing that God equips the one He calls.

"Now may the God of Peace ... equip you with everything good for doing His will" (Hebrews 13:20-21).

So, we began meeting in Yateley and Basingstoke on alternate weeks until such time as we felt confident enough to go it alone. Christine was invaluable initially, as a co-leader, before her untimely death only months later, but not before the Lord provided another co-leader, Jenny, who turned out to be my right hand.

Jenny's practical skills, stemming from years of teaching were extremely useful especially in various projects, which we undertook in bringing to life well-known scripture such as 'The Christmas Story.' The retelling of 'The Christmas Story' was my first attempt at presenting in a novel way what can be for some the all-too-familiar story of the birth of Christ. A fresh approach was needed, I thought.

Taking an idea from the Medieval Mystery Plays, Jenny and I constructed a stage built from milk crates on which a plywood top was fixed. Over this, we draped a dark cloth, placing on it a tableau depicting the birth scene, using the figures of Mary, Joseph and the infant Jesus borrowed from the church's nativity crib. To create the atmosphere of this lowly scene, Anne Thal, a professional potter who had recently joined the group, fashioned forty or fifty footlights made from clay in the style of hand-held lamps similar to those used during the time of Christ. These were lit immediately prior to the audience being quietly led into the darkened hall, save for these lamps. To one side of the stage were two readers. The first would read the narrative, as recorded in Scripture, while the second reader drew attention to the possible thoughts and feelings of Mary and Joseph. Prayerful reflection followed as the story progressed to provoke an inner response from the audience. The approach proved so popular that night that we adopted it in the telling of the 'The Woman at the Well' liturgy sometime later.

It was also through Jenny that Irene came into the group. Jenny knew Irene through a pottery class run by Anne Thal mentioned above. Anne had a strong conversion on her first visit. Initially coming for healing prayer for a broken arm which was not improving, the Lord knew she needed more than her arm to be fixed and touched her heart in the place she needed it. After thirty-five years away from Church, Anne came back to faith that night and her arm healed quite naturally.

Soon Mary W, joined us and became a faithful member for many years, likewise Mary P-B. So, the chain of faith grew, in length and strength. Despite this, the group was never too large to fit comfortably in my lounge. Usually, members stayed for two to three years, leaving only to set up prayer groups in their respective parishes, then another member or two would join and do likewise. This seemed to be God's plan. Apart from Jenny, only one other person, Louise joined from our parish. I could not discern the pattern at the time, but looking back, I can see that the Lord was spreading renewal thinly but widely. Representatives from most of the parishes in the deanery made their way to our hearth, then He sent them out in twos to ignite renewal in their own parishes.

"Calling the Twelve to Him, He began to send them out two by two" (Mark 6:7)

Another member of the Prayer Group was Kay, who I had first met at a seminar about The Second Vatican Council, so I was delighted when we were reconnected at the Basingstoke Day of Renewal. Soon, she became a very supportive member of the Yateley group as well, occasionally using her gift of prophecy to bring messages of encouragement from the Lord.

I could relate many amazing stories about those wonderful ten years of the group's duration, some of which are sprinkled throughout this book, but this is not within the remit of this reflection. However, because he was the only man to be influenced by the prayer group, I cannot conclude without telling the story of the part which the group played in my husband Tom's conversion.

For years we had been praying for Tom's return to faith and for him to receive the Baptism in the Holy Spirit. Nevertheless, each Wednesday evening, he would go to the pub with our neighbour, Chris, returning when the meeting had finished. One evening, Chris was late. Tom stood peering into the living room while waiting for the usual knock on the door heralding Chris' arrival. Then, he slipped quietly into the room, taking a seat nearest the door. By the time Chris arrived, we were about fifteen minutes into the meeting, and Tom had stayed!

The following week, Tom went through the same ritual of slipping into the room and taking a seat, but this time there was a different outcome. I could hardly believe my ears at the discourse between the two men, as Tom opened the door. "I'm not going tonight, Chris. I'm joining the prayer meeting!" Chris could hardly believe his ears, too, and chuckled inanely. From then on, a new night had to be found for the customary visit to the pub and Tom joined the Prayer Group every week whenever he was home from a trip and, later, he returned to the faith. Soon, he started to use his trips abroad to shop around the Catholic bookshops, especially in Chicago, where there were numerous biblical resources. From these, I was later able to teach the group. Tom, meanwhile, had become interested in all things Jewish and the development of Christianity from its Jewish roots. It was Tom who introduced us all to the Passover Meal and he took great pleasure in leading it. The Lord held the group together for ten years, until a new decade dawned, and with it a new direction for my life, a decade filled with study for new ministries.

BEAUTIFUL BERMUDA
August 1981

It always gave Tom great pleasure to introduce the family to some of the beautiful destinations he visited during trips. Bermuda had become a firm favourite of his, so when he first mentioned the idea of taking the family to visit, there was great excitement at the prospect. I knew very little about Bermuda. Most people had heard of the famous Bermuda Triangle and all the legends associated with it, of the many ships which had mysteriously disappeared and aeroplanes that had vanished without trace. All this added to the attraction of our holiday, although I did feel a little apprehensive about flying over it ourselves!

Since we were travelling on a concessionary ticket (courtesy of BA) there was the usual anxious wait at the check-in desk to see if there were seats available. It was rather optimistic to expect there to be five seats to accommodate the whole family, especially to such an exotic destination, and sure enough, there were only two available seats that day. We were crestfallen initially, but then it was decided that Stephen and I should take up these seats and the rest of the family would hopefully follow the next day.

On arrival in Bermuda, we made our way to a Guest House called Salt Kettle in the district of Paget, where we received a very warm welcome from our host, a woman of English descent, who prided herself on her English connection. Being good British subjects, she told us, Bermudians celebrated Empire Day, (now called Commonwealth Day), the Queen's Birthday, Guy Fawkes Day; and they drive on the left-hand side of the road, which was very convenient for us.

We arrived about noon. After lunch, we settled ourselves near the small inlet, both of us seeking shelter from the sun, sitting under a nearby tree. Thus, we spent our first hours, awaiting the arrival of the rest of the family. Thankfully, they did manage to get a seat on the plane the next day and we were joyfully re-united. But Stephen and I looked as if we were from a different family. Despite our best efforts to keep in the shade, we had each turned bright pink!

With the family complete, the holiday had begun, and we lost no time in arranging our means of exploring the island. There were no rental cars in those days, to prevent too much traffic in the delightful narrow streets and roads of the island. Taxis may be used for tourists' transportation, but this would prove too expensive and would be rather inhibitive for Tom's sense of exploration. But bicycles and Mobylettes (mopeds) could be rented, which we duly did. Peter was still too young to ride one of his own, so he rode pillion on Stephen's, I rode pillion with Tom and Anne rode one of her own. I mention this mode of transport because it features later in my recollections.

If you can tear yourself away from the sun-splashed beaches, there is plenty to see and do in Bermuda. Golf, fishing, sailing and diving are all very popular as are many other sports and the landscape is rich in natu-

Pauline, Tom. Stephen and Peter with moped Bermuda 1981

ral beauty. What struck me was the immense pride the residents took in the upkeep of their beautifully painted homes and manicured lawns. Bermudian homes have been described as basically English cottages adapted to the specific and unique conditions existing in Bermuda. Typically white-roofed and painted in pale hues of pink and blue, Bermuda's houses give a tropical appearance, particularly when they have gardens aflame with a variety of colours from the many beautiful flowers.

Exploring the island as we duly did on our mopeds, we came across the most stunning sea views, lovely beaches, hidden coves and beautiful gardens along the country lanes.

Many people choose to take a boat trip of some form or other to cruise around the island or to explore the reefs and wrecks below the sea. We took a trip by glass bottom boat and were fascinated to see shoals of fish of all colours swimming beneath our boat.

On the other side of Paget to Salt Kettle was Hamilton Harbour, a popular disembarkation point for many international cruise ships. When I first saw the cruise ships nestling alongside the harbour, I never thought for an instant that I would ever be fortunate enough to go on a cruise. I was to wait another thirty years for that privilege.

We very much enjoyed visiting the town of St George's, which was the original capital of Bermuda until the government was transferred to Hamilton in 1815. St. George's was founded in 1612 and our visit there was very much like stepping back in time to the seventeenth century. Many of the buildings had been carefully and sensitively restored to their original architecture and they certainly added to the town's charm and character, with its picturesque cottages and cobbled lanes. Bermuda is very proud of its historical past, and we learned that every Wednesday, from November to February, visitors to St George's are personally greeted by the town's major. Then, just before noon, the Bermuda Regiment, complete with drums and bugles, marches into the Town Square before the traditional noonday cannon salute is fired.

Replicas of the stocks and pillory used for punishment in the seventeenth century had been placed in King's Square. Yes, we took the usual tourist pictures of the kids in the stocks! Here, too, we saw a Town Crier, used to lend atmosphere to the scene, and a ducking stool, where the unfortunate wench accused of witchcraft was duly ducked.

Another interesting piece of history is Gibb's Hill Lighthouse, which was built on one of the highest points of the island and has been in operation since 1846. It is one of the most powerful lights of the world's shipping lanes and we were told that aircraft can see its flashes from over one

Sons Peter (left) and Stephen (right) in the stocks, Bermuda 1981

hundred miles (160 kilometres) away.

It soon became obvious to us all why Bermuda was such a favourite trip for Tom. We all enjoyed the holiday immensely and I am sure we all stored up our own favourite memories. It must have made a favourable impression, because in later years, both Stephen and Anne holidayed there with their respective spouses. Tom and I also returned when our children had left home.

Speaking of special memories, what I would now like to share is what for me was the most spectacular memory of our family holiday.

It was the last full day of the holiday and Tom was anxious to check if we had seats on the flight to New York, where we had a two-night stopover planned, before returning to London. This involved his having to go to the airport to make enquiries. To make best use of the remaining time we had, I took the kids to the beach.

To put what follows next into context, since the profound experience of the Baptism in the Holy Spirit, I found myself avidly reading the Bible. However, I was confused and apprehensive because of a chance remark by our priest to the effect that "You can't be let loose on the Scriptures - you might misinterpret them."

Once the kids were happily occupied on the beach, I found myself musing on this and, before I knew it, my musing had turned into prayer, addressed to 'My Father' which was another aspect of my earlier encounter with the Holy Spirit. No longer was 'God' a remote concept, but He had become a living reality and now I found myself addressing Him as Father, reflecting our newfound relationship, through the power of the Holy Spirit.

Childlike, I poured out my heart, with its confusion. I wanted to know, specifically, if the Holy Scriptures were indeed God's Word and could I trust them as His word? How silly, I thought. How can God answer such a prayer?

Just at that moment, I remembered having read somewhere that the most important part of prayer is not what we say to God, but what He says to us. But how does God speak to us? I thought. I did not consider myself so favoured as to actually hear from God directly.

As if in answer to this thought, I had a flashback to a conversation with a neighbour of mine, Joyce, whose daughter played with my daughter, Anne. Joyce's opening comment surprised me with, "Your Anne hangs on every word you say, doesn't she?" "Does she?" I exclaimed in surprise. Then, Joyce recalled how one day she had overheard the two girls disagreeing about something and, so the story goes, Anne, in a gesture of settling the dispute once and for all, placed her hands confidently on her hips, and, taking a stand, said 'Well, **my** mum says…" (as if to say, "so that settles it!"). To say I was flabbergasted would be an understatement. We do not realise how much we influence our children, do we? Nor do we appreciate how much our words are sinking in.

With this recall, I took up my prayer to God once again, with, "Yes Father, that's the kind of confidence I want when reading your Word. Just as Anne had confidence in my words to her, I want that kind of confidence in reading the Bible. Is it really your Word? I need to know that I can trust the Bible to be your Word because I want a faith that is solidly based."

Then I remembered something else I had read. The guidelines on prayer suggested waiting for fifteen minutes after praying in order to hear what God is saying to you. This was not a reassuring thought because I was not accustomed to praying in this manner and questioned in my mind whether it could be as simple as that.

After a little while, my thoughts were interrupted by the sound of Tom's voice calling me on his return from the airport. The news was good - there were enough seats for us all to travel together.

After issuing this news, he said he had a little 'pressie' for me. Intrigued, I waited as he struggled slightly to extract something from the back pocket of his jeans, which he duly passed over to me. It was the size of a bus ticket, with a corner torn off, and had a silver background on which there was blue writing. I read the inscription in utter disbelief and shock, for it was the perfect answer to my prayer offered only moments ago: It had a cross at the top, followed underneath by the words:

God said it,
I believe it,
That settles it!

After my initial shock and excitement at this timely answer to my earlier prayer, I enquired how Tom had acquired it. The story gets even weirder here. His explanation was that as he was riding along the road on the moped, something glinted up at him, blinding him momentarily, which aroused his curiosity sufficiently to stop to see what it was. His immediate thought on reading it was "That's for Pauline!"

This was not to be the only time he was to be the messenger from God for me.

As you can imagine that little token became, and still is, my most prized possession and its message has served me well over the years in approaching the Bible with due reverence, as God's word.

Yes, beautiful Bermuda will always have a very special place in my heart.

Thank you, dear Heavenly Father for that special gift!

HEALING AT RUE DU BAC
13 February 1982

Conversion as a process not an event, is borne out very clearly in what I am about to share, but before embarking upon the highlight of this episode of my life, I need to take you way back to how my 'problem' with Our Lady began.

I attended Catholic schools in the late 1940s to mid-1950s, when devotion to Our Lady was very popular. In my parish, as in most, one particular devotion was the crowning of Our Lady's statue on the first Sunday of May, the month dedicated to Her. The child chosen for this great honour was usually from the reception class, selection based on the child with a perfect school attendance record.

This process eliminated any chance of my being selected, because in my first year of school, I had contracted numerous illnesses, resulting in a poor attendance record. As an only child up to the age of seven, I had been shielded from most illnesses but once I was exposed to other children, I contracted most of the common childhood diseases, even the greatly feared Diphtheria!

In later years, having passed the Eleven-plus examination, I was offered a place at a single-sex Convent High

School named after St Joseph, established by The Sisters of Charity. Our teachers were a mixture of laity and nuns from this Order, but the Headmistress was a nun named Sister Margaret.

It was a tradition of the school for us to undergo a two-year period of formation to become a consecrated 'Child of Mary,' a guild to which we could subscribe throughout our life if we so wished. The ethos of the guild was to model our life and morals on the purity and sanctity of the Blessed Mother. We received formation lessons during lunchtime, and I attended these with enthusiasm. Then, through an unfortunate set of circumstances, my mother, already suffering from Rheumatoid Arthritis, became so disabled and unwell that I had to stay at home from school to look after her needs and to assume many domestic duties. At the time, my father's employment in the building trade took him away from home from Monday to Saturday afternoon, and as my only sibling was a brother aged seven, most of the burden fell upon my shoulders. Thus, I spent most of the next year dodging between attending school and caring for my mother.

School was unaware of my home situation I hasten to add. Notes were sent into school to excuse my absences purporting that I was unwell, because it was illegal to keep a child from school, no matter how desperate the situation. Indeed, a parent could go to prison for this offence.

On more than one occasion, I remember the School Board official knocking on the front door to enquire about my absences. Aware of the seriousness of the situation, I had to hide among the layers of coats hanging behind the front door in case he should peep through the lace curtains at the front window and perhaps see me!

As a result of my absences, which, of course, affected my Formation Classes as well as my general education, the day of reckoning eventually came round and one day I was informed by Sister Monica that because of my many absences, I could not be put forward for Consecration to the Guild of The Children of Mary. However, I could re-apply next year.

What a blow! For a second time, once through my own illness and now because of my mother's illness, I was not considered acceptable through no fault of my own. Apart from feelings of rejection, humiliation and resentment, I was angry at the injustice of the decision, as I saw it, and subconsciously projected my anger onto Our Lady. To have blamed my mother in any way would have been unthinkable, so from that moment, I was indifferent to the whole notion of 'belonging' to Mary. I would do quite well without Her! With such thoughts, my heart began progressively to harden towards Her.

Fast forward now to me in my early fifties. By this time, I had experienced a deep conversion accompanied by 'Baptism in the Holy Spirit' and was leading a small prayer group in my home every Wednesday evening. Everything was going favourably until a new member joined us, who had what I considered a fanatical devotion to Our Lady and, quite frankly, I saw her well-meaning interventions as a distraction, which irritated me enormously. I did not understand then why this should annoy me so much but I asked the Lord to show me the source of my malcontent, and to heal me of whatever caused me to feel this way. In response, I felt the Lord say that He wanted me to get to know His Mother. With my compliance to God's will, I resolved to open myself up to the Lord's revelation and possible healing in this regard.

When this particular member of the group invited me to go with her to Lourdes on her annual pilgrimage, I thought perhaps this was where I might find healing, so I agreed to accompany her.

It was a short, two-day pilgrimage, arriving in Lourdes for the Feast Day, 11th February. I was introduced to the usual activities there, especially bathing in and drinking the water from the miraculous spring, which had sprung up when St Bernadette, at the request of the 'Beautiful Lady' was instructed to "go and wash." At first, the instructions seemed implausible because there was only soil in that area, but as Bernadette continued to grovel in the dirt and go through the motions of washing, suddenly a slow trickle of water appeared, eventually developing into a spring, which has flowed to this day. Subsequently, the first miracles were reported and people flocked with their sick.

Lourdes as a place of pilgrimage and healing grew so quickly it soon outstripped the basilica, which was originally built on the instruction of Our Lady. Over time, an underground basilica accommodating 25,000 pilgrims had to be built to protect the pilgrims from inclement weather.

Lourdes has been a place of pilgrimage for hundreds of

thousands since 1858 and many miracles have been authenticated by the Church. Many cures are not even submitted for the process of authentication by the Church. For those people 'proof' doesn't seem necessary. They just 'know' and give thanks to God, Our Lady, and St Bernadette.

I personally know of two individuals who have received miraculous healings at Lourdes, one the daughter of a friend, from a brain tumour, the other from a condition in the jaw which is described as 'suicide pain.' I do not know the medical term for the condition, but to this day it is incurable. I know this from the experience of another friend whose husband has the same condition. Why some should be cured whilst others are not is a mystery to us, but faith tells us God has a purpose.

My stay in Lourdes passed quickly, and I was a little disappointed that nothing remarkable appeared to have occurred, so it was with a somewhat heavy heart that we set off on our return, a long, seventeen-hour overland journey.

Many hours passed and day turned into nightfall just as we were approaching the outskirts of Paris. I was tired and was just falling asleep when the driver announced we were going to stop shortly at a famous church, Rue du Bac, another place of pilgrimage where Our Lady was said to have appeared.

By the time we arrived, I was feeling so exhausted I decided to stay on the coach. But then, I felt a nudge from the Holy Spirit that I should make an effort and go inside so I joined the group, and we entered La Rue du Bac Church. As seasoned pilgrims do, I picked up some leaflets at the

*St.Catherine Laboure's incorrupt
body lying in glass casket*

back of the church to read later, since we were only allowed a short time at this stop.

We were guided down the left-hand aisle leading to the side altar, below which was a crystal casket in which lay the incorrupt body of a nun, whom I would later learn was Saint Catherine Laboure.

It was her habit which first caught my attention, especially the cornice, a large, pointed headgear with winged sides. I knew it well from school. St Catherine was, apparently, from the same Order as my nuns, the Sisters of Charity! What is more, she looked so like my own Sister Monica who had taken me for Formation Classes as an Aspirant of The Children of Mary Guild. This was the first shock.

Slowly, we moved towards the centre of the church, directly in front of the tabernacle, above which was a large statue of Our Lady, which I recognised as the famous image on the 'Miraculous Medal', which the Children of Mary wore, suspended from a blue satin ribbon.

Later, when I had an opportunity, I opened the leaflets to learn something of the history of the church, which apparently had been built on the very spot where Sister Catherine Laboure, a Sister of Charity affiliated to St Vincent de Paul, had an apparition of Our Blessed Lady in 1830. Sister Catherine, as she was then called, was instructed by Our Lady to

St Catherine Laboure and the miraculous medal

request the local bishop to have a medal struck depicting Her image, just as she appeared to Sister Catherine, holding out Her hands in a gesture of offering, from which streams of light were radiating. Around the oval medal shape of the apparition were the words, *"O Mary, conceived without sin, pray for us who have recourse to Thee."*

This prayer was later used to support the Dogma of The Immaculate Conception, and was as similarly revealed to St Bernadette at Lourdes in 1858 when on the eighteenth and final apparition Our Lady eventually identified Herself with the words: *"I am the Immaculate Conception."*

To the poorly educated Bernadette, these words would have been totally incomprehensible, but she remembered them only by repeating them over and over to herself as she made her way to the priest's house. This statement from a simple peasant girl is what finally convinced the priest to sit up and take her claims seriously.

When a medal was subsequently struck to commemorate the revelation given to Sister Catherine, the title initially given to the Apparition was 'Our Lady of Graces', which the rays from Her hands depicted. The medal quickly became popularly known as 'The Miraculous Medal' after many miracles, stories of healing and conversion were attributed to the devotion of wearing the medal and praying for Our Lady's intercession.

A further explanation about the rays caught my attention

with considerable force. When Sister Catherine Laboure asked why some of the rays were radiantly lit whilst others remained dull, Our Lady explained that the lighted ones represented the graces she was allowed to bestow upon those who asked for Her intercession, whilst the dull ones represented the people who did not ask for Her intercession.

Time was getting short, and we would be leaving the church soon, but this explanation struck home so forcefully that I quickly returned to the main altar directly in front of the tabernacle. I knew what I must do. There, asking Jesus to forgive me for rejecting the wonderful gift of His Mother, and at the same time asking Our Lady to be my spiritual Mother, I was comforted with the words, "You are indeed a Child of Mary." The privilege and dignity I had denied myself for so many years was restored in that instant.

So, my trip to Lourdes had not been in vain after all. As so often happened in later episodes of my life, the Lord worked His miracle at the eleventh hour. Further insights surfaced as I reflected on the wonderful tapestry the Lord was weaving with my life to bring about the healing of long-standing painful memories.

We arrived at Rue du Bac on 13th February, the date of the apparition to Saint Catherine who was from the same Order of nuns as the nuns who taught me, namely The Sisters of Charity.

The incorrupt body of Saint Catherine dressed in the same habit as our Sister Monica who took the Formation classes to become a Child of Mary, brought back painful memories of being rejected.

The explanation of the unlit rays convinced me of my need of healing, and I was given the grace of repentance, healing, and acceptance. That very date, 13th February, was the date of my mother's death.

The wound of rejection caused by my mother's illness also died that day. Thereafter, a new relationship began to develop between the Blessed Mother and me.

More recently, in 2017, whilst attending a conference in Birmingham, I was sitting at a dining table next to another delegate, when I noticed her Liverpool accent and commented on it. Since my whole family was originally from Liverpool, we had some common ground on which to start a conversation. During the short time we had together I mentioned about my daughter Anne's recently diagnosed breast cancer.

Just then Supper was finishing, and the evening's entertainment was about to start, but before leaving to return to our original conference seats, the lady rummaged into her bag and brought out two Miraculous Medals, suspended on blue thread, offering one for me and one for Anne.

At last, I had received my Miraculous Medal and that simple gesture made me feel finally and officially consecrated as a 'Child of Mary.'

"You have saved the best till now" (John 2:10)

JERUSALEM

JERUSALEM FOR A DAY
21 December 1982

Christmas plans were well underway; Anne and Stephen were already home from university for the Christmas holiday and Tom was free from flying duties for the period. It was going to be a quiet, uneventful time. Then the letter from Jerusalem dropped through our letter box.

Earlier in the year I had attended a Leaders' Charismatic Conference at LSU (La Sainte Union) in Southampton, where, for the second time, I met the Pentecostal Minister, Sister Ruth Heflin. Nearly always dressed in white, she was a very imposing figure and a dynamic speaker with a voice to match. As one friend once commented, "Her voice could open London Bridge!" But Ruth had more than a dynamic speaking voice; she also had the charismatic Gift of Prophecy. On her first visit to our Conference, we had all been stunned by the anecdotes she told of the many journeys to various parts of the world which she had undertaken and, after going in faith, amazing events would unfold.

At the time, she said that during the following year, some of us at the Conference would also experience being called in like manner. I remember this distinctly and knew intuitively the words were for me. Now, an invitation to Jerusalem had arrived.

On the face of it, it was just a polite 'keeping in touch' round-robin sort of letter, addressed to "Dear Friends." It was an invitation to join Ruth's community, The Mount Zion Fellowship in Jerusalem, for what was described as 'Christmas Open House' on 21st December. Out of the question, I thought, but then I read the letter again.

My first reaction was that Ruth had sent the same letter to people she had come to know a little at the Conference, but on making enquiries amongst the group which accompanied me I soon learned this was not so. Reading the letter again it seemed rather less like a round-robin and more like a genuine invitation, especially when the "Dear Friends" was superseded with a personally written note, ending with the words, "Hope to see you." My third thought was perhaps this was somehow connected with Ruth's prophecy that some of us would be 'called' and tested by our response.

I did not have long to make a decision if I were to try to accept the invitation, which would entail a lot of explaining to my boss for requesting time off at such short notice, to say nothing of explaining it all to Tom, plus the difficulty of securing a concessionary airline ticket to Tel Aviv at one of the busiest times of the year.

After gaining Tom's support and cooperation in this venture, the next thing to check was whether I had any holiday leave left to cover the three days I would need; a day to travel, a day in Jerusalem for 'Open House' and a day to return. Checking with Personnel, I learned I had four days left. Getting a ticket would prove a little harder. All flights on and around the 21st were fully booked, but then the Lord began to work on my behalf. In the meantime, I had decided to take Anne with me.

With time quickly running out, Tom decided to go directly to 'Crew Reporting' to request two tickets for Anne and me on 20th December and was just being turned down because there was only one spare seat. Just then, a pilot who was checking in, overheard the conversation between the check-in clerk and Tom and interrupted, overriding the clerk's words saying, "Book them on, that's my flight. I'm on duty that day." Phew! But then another potential problem surfaced. There was no return flight from Tel Aviv on 22nd but there was a flight on 23rd and with two seats available. Thank God for His provision once again and thank goodness I had an extra day's holiday left to cover the extended stay!

The day of our departure duly arrived, and Tom drove us to the airport and helped us navigate our way around. Finally making our way to the cabin, the stewardess was looking out for us to show us to a seat in First Class, but as she explained, one of us would have to use the jump seat (a cockpit seat usually reserved for an additional crew member or a training instructor). Anne was delighted at this prospect, and I settled happily into the First-Class seat the Lord had providentially reserved for me!

By the time we arrived in Tel Aviv, dusk was settling and the light fading. It took us quite a while to work out how to get from Tel Aviv to Jerusalem, but finally, by means of bus and taxi, we arrived at Halcyon House, which was a gated residence. During the bus journey from Tel Aviv, we passed through many small towns and villages and what was conspicuous to me was the contrast with the Christmas lights back home, where almost every house was brightly lit with numerous lights; in contrast, driving along to Jerusalem we rarely saw a display of lights in the windows. Most were in darkness.

Several Scriptures readily came to mind as we trundled along:

"As He approached Jerusalem and saw the city, He wept over it and said, If you, even you, had only known on this day what would bring peace – but now it is hidden from your eyes... because you did not recognise the time of God's coming to you." (Luke 19:41-42, 44)

How often have I reflected on Our Lord weeping over Jerusalem because the people did not recognise the time of His visitation, when He, God's Son, Jesus Christ, the long-awaited Messiah was in their midst; He who said of Himself,

"I am the Light of the World. Whoever follows me will never walk in darkness but will have the light of life." (John 8:12).

Yet to this day the Jewish people are still in darkness. These reflections also called to mind our host in Jerusalem,

Ruth Heflin, who left her home in Ashland, Virginia, spending most of her life abroad, firstly in Hong Kong and eventually Jerusalem, answering the call to 'Pray for the peace of Jerusalem' and to stand by and pray for the Jewish people's return to their homeland. She believed firmly that their present blindness would one day be restored, as in the case of St Paul.

"It was as though scales immediately fell away from his eyes and immediately, he was able to see again"
(NJ Acts 9:18).

These were some of my thoughts as the bus rumbled on towards Jerusalem. By the time we reached Halcyon House it was 10 pm and initially our attempts at rousing the community were unsuccessful but, eventually, a community member unlocked a series of locks and bolts and opened up for us, welcoming us in. After eating a simple supper, we were shown to our bedrooms, promising us that we would see Ruth at breakfast.

Next morning, we joined Ruth and the community for breakfast, and she was clearly delighted that we had responded to her invitation to attend their 'Open House'. After breakfast, she directed one of her colleagues to take us on a whirlwind tour of Jerusalem, while she and the rest of the community completed preparations for 'Open House' in the evening.

By the time Anne and I arrived back from our tour of some of the major sites we were quite exhausted, so after a light meal we took some rest in readiness for the evening celebrations. We still did not know what to expect and were kept in suspense until we all met in the large lounge at 7 pm.

Ruth had become so highly regarded during her time in Jerusalem that key representatives from the major religions: Jews, Christians and Muslims, usually attended the annual Open House. The Mayor of Jerusalem, as well as other civic dignitaries also attended and it was a privilege to be introduced to some of these that night. Shortly after introductions and a welcome were completed, the music started, and Anne and I were quickly swept up by the lively melodies and dancing.

Pauline with Ruth Heflin (left) in Jerusalem-1982

The evening passed all too quickly, and it was fun listening to Ruth and her colleagues reminiscing later about the evening and some stories they had heard. We felt privileged to be part of their intimacies.

Just before we finally adjourned for the evening, we were told the plans for the next day. We were all to visit several villages in Lebanon. I thanked God again for turning an initial disappointment, a day's delay in leaving Jerusalem, into what turned out to be one of the most joyful and memorable memories of our brief stay. So, this was why we had had to stay on an extra day, and why I happened to have that extra day's leave!

The next day we had an exciting time travelling together

in the coach, singing lovely praise songs, to Ruth's accompaniment on the accordion. This was not at all my image of a missionary!

Lebanon was quite a shock. The houses were very poorly constructed and there were obvious signs of houses having been shelled or bombed, yet there was a very warm welcome from waving villagers as they heard the music issuing from our vehicle as we passed their way.

Eventually, we reached our destination, a village church, and were quickly hurried inside as the service was about to start. At the end of the official service, The Mount Zion Fellowship was invited to take their place on the make-shift stage, myself and Anne included. With Ruth's accompaniment once again, we sang a medley of Christmas carols.

I must have recently seen *The Sound of Music* because the occasion reminded me of the scene in the film when the Von Trapp family were singing just before their escape over the mountains!

From there we went from village to village singing in the local churches, humbled by their obvious appreciation of the little we had to offer. What a day! The Lord certainly had stored up a great treat for us.

Soon we were to return home, but before going to bed that night, Ruth and a few of the community gathered round for a short time of prayer to send Anne and me on our way back home. It was then, in one of Ruth's prophetic utterances, that the reason for the call to Jerusalem was revealed. The purpose was in preparation for other callings, a time of testing to see if I would respond to God's call without necessarily understanding the reason for it.

Just before our departure the next morning, we were each presented with a wall plaque to remind us of our special Christmas visit to their 'Open House.'

Left: Plaque given to Anne by Ruth Heflin in Jerusalem 1982
Right: Plaque given to Pauline by Ruth Heflin in Jerusalem 1982

SURPRISE AT THE
ROYAL ALBERT HALL
16 July 1983

Following my Christmas visit to Halcyon House in Jerusalem, I started to receive regular newsletters from the
community, which were especially interesting and kept me
up to date with Ruth's travels. It was in one such newsletter
where I learned that Ruth was bringing over with her a
well-known Rabbi and singer, Schlomo Carlebach to appear
with her at The Royal Albert Hall, London, later in the year.
I was thrilled at the news and immediately began planning
to take a group to see my remarkable new-found friend.

Over time I became more and more acquainted with
Ruth, even spending a week in Jerusalem living with the
fellowship and seeing what was meant by 'living by faith.'
As far as I could see, they lived very frugally and did not
appear to have any regular means of income, save for contri-
butions from family and friends back home in Virginia, who
supported Ruth's vision of bringing Christ to the nations,
and especially to the Jewish people. Donations when Ruth
spoke at conferences brought in an added source of income,
but these were quickly absorbed in travel costs to which-
ever part of the world the Lord wished her to go. I was

tremendously impressed by their deep faith and trust that the Lord would provide all their needs. Often, however, the answer to their prayer came only at the eleventh hour, which seemed only to strengthen their faith.

Ruth's reputation as a gifted speaker was well known among Pentecostal and Evangelical circles and during the week that I stayed with her in Ashland she took me to one of her speaking engagements in Washington. The occasion was a Men's Breakfast, held at one of the most prestigious hotels in the city, hosted by an Evangelical organisation called 'The Full Gospel Businessmen's Fellowship International.'

How, I thought, had Ruth managed to be invited to appear at The Royal Albert Hall? A clue came at one of the conferences I attended. Ruth was full of stories and anecdotes, and during some of these she mentioned a special friend, a certain Lady Astor, one of several rich American heiresses who married into English aristocracy. She and Ruth had somehow become friends and it was she who had arranged for Ruth and the Rabbi to appear at The Royal Albert Hall. How their friendship began I do not know but I believe that it was Lady Astor who was responsible for arranging this occasion.

Ruth's own story was very interesting. Having been raised by two parents who were both Pentecostal ministers, it came as no surprise that their two children, Ruth and her brother Wallace Heflin Jnr, should both follow in their footsteps and likewise become Pentecostal ministers.

Unlike her parents who stayed in Virginia, Ruth initially felt called to the nations and in fact wrote her own song entitled, *I Ask For The Nations*. At the age of eighteen, she went to Hong Kong, became proficient in Cantonese and was able to preach to the underground churches. She stayed there many years and set up a fellowship, which would one day be the launching pad for when the door to China was open. Meanwhile, they served the Vietnamese boat people - people surging out of Vietnam to escape the civil war.

Ruth's call to Jerusalem came at some stage in her thirties and she remained there for the rest of her life, with intermittent missionary journeys to many parts of the world for the Lord. She eventually became an internationally known speaker, hence her invitation to the Southampton conference I attended and now to the Royal Albert Hall. Her connection with Lady Astor does not seem so odd, given this little summary of Ruth's life.

So many people had heard of Ruth through me that I soon had enough names to warrant booking a large coach to transport us to London. The week of the event was also another singularly important one for our family. Our eldest child, Stephen, was due to graduate the day before the Royal Albert Hall event. My father had travelled from Manchester, and we were all looking forward to witnessing this historic event for our family. Stephen was the first one from either side of the family to gain a university degree and we were so proud of him.

During the week of the graduation, my father became unwell with a chest infection, and I had been pricked by a rose bush thorn, which became infected, resulting in cellulitis. When my leg swelled to nearly twice its normal size, we called the doctor who checked out both my father and me, and prescribed appropriate medications, with instructions for me to keep my leg raised.

As the week progressed, it became apparent I would not be able to attend Stephen's graduation, nor the occasion at the Royal Albert Hall. I was devastated on both counts, but it left me with the worrying responsibility of cancelling the coach and refunding the coach money to everyone.

Thankfully, the graduation day went well, with just Tom attending. The following day was still a problem. Then the situation took a positive turn. I had awoken that morning minus the fever which had accompanied the illness for the past few days. Nevertheless, I still couldn't put my foot to the ground let alone stand on it or walk. Noticing how much better I seemed, Tom asked if I would still go if he could manage to get hold of a wheelchair! "Too true," I said and a quick call to the Red Cross found Tom on his way to collect one. Soon the group bundled itself into the coach and we were off!

Not knowing if there were a special entrance for wheelchairs, we arrived in good time and duly joined the queue. After a while, an attendant spotted me and directed Tom and my father to another entrance, where we were transported in a lift up to the back row of the nearest section to the stage.

Eventually, the singing Rabbi and his small accompanying band opened the afternoon's proceedings, engaging everyone with his lively songs. Finally, it was Ruth's turn to be introduced and she opened with her signature tune *I Ask*

For The Nations. This was followed by one or two stories and anecdotes about her call to Jerusalem and the fascinating stories reported by Jewish people of seeing Jesus, Messiah walking along the ramparts of the remaining 'Western' 'or 'Wailing' Wall. I must add here that Rabbi Schlomo was himself a believer in Jesus, Messiah.

At a certain point, Ruth stepped down from the stage to pray for a line of people who had indicated they wished her to pray for them. I knew from experience that before a significant event such as this, Ruth would have fasted and prayed for many days in order to receive a special anointing of the Holy Spirit to impart to those whom the Lord wished to bless through her hands.

Moving to the end of the line of people, Ruth lightly touched the forehead of the first person and the whole row of about ten people immediately and simultaneously fell down, 'resting in the Spirit' where they stayed for several minutes. Then Ruth began swiftly moving through the people, touching as many as she could reach while this incredible anointing was on her.

Ruth then moved towards the section we were in, climbing the stairs and reaching out on either side of the aisle, to bless as many people as she could. As she reached the last row where I was sitting, still in the wheelchair, Ruth came up to me, only recognising me at that point. I remember her gasping in surprise at the recognition. She started to ask why I was in a wheelchair, but before I could explain, the power of Holy Spirit overwhelmed me, and I too rested in the Spirit for several minutes. My first recollection on coming round, was that my right foot was tapping, and I knew I wanted to dance for joy in gratitude.

Without a moment's hesitation, I got out of the chair, made my way down the aisle and onto the stage, where I danced and twirled in thanksgiving for God's surprise gift of healing! Later, when we finally met up with the rest of our group, I was pushing the wheelchair and did so all the way to where the coach was parked. My leg was completely healed.

DO WHATEVER HE TELLS YOU
13 August 1983

I had never kept a diary as such, save for spiritual jottings to remind me of how the Lord has guided and sometimes intervened in my life from time to time, so I did not anticipate the event which occurred during the early hours of 13th August 1983.

As far as I recall, I was awakened from sleep by an audible voice sounding in my ears, speaking the words, *"Thou shalt write of Me and of My work in thee."*

I was immediately alert and sitting on the side of my bed, when I heard the words repeated, spoken in a compelling yet non-threatening voice, which I knew intuitively to be God the Father speaking!

Anxious to write down these words lest I should forget them by morning (as if I could), I slipped out of bed and made my way down the stairs to get writing materials with which to record the message.

To my astonishment, and as if to reassure me that I had not dreamed the whole thing, the voice took up again, by which time I was practically tumbling down the stairs so as not to miss a single word. The voice came again, just as before, with the additional words, *"Thy pen shall flow in My Word."*

The next morning, I looked at the words. This had certainly happened, but what was I to make of the message? What were these "works?" I had experienced God's marvellous intervention in my life on several occasions already. Were these perhaps what the Lord wanted me to write down?

What especially struck me about this experience was how I knew intuitively that it was God the Father speaking to me. As if to emphasise this, the date this occurred was 13th August 1983 - my own earthly father's birthday!

Another thing which puzzled me was the use of 'thee and thou." If my subconscious were making this up, I never would have used these pronouns. I most certainly would have used "you."

Speaking about this with a group of people at a Conference the following year, (it happened to be the anniversary of my hearing the message) one member of the group gave a possible explanation. "Thee" and "thou" are intimate pronouns used within a family context and especially by a parent to a child. (I knew this from learning French). God the Father was speaking as a parent to me, His child! This sounded plausible to me then and I have not found a better explanation, so I am staying with that.

Now, to come back to the title I have given to this reflection. Over the years, I have been rather haunted by the fact that I have not carried out this instruction, but occasionally one or two of my anecdotes have leaked out in family gatherings and my grandchildren have urged me to "write it down." In addition, the long months of Covid restrictions and lockdown have given me the opportunity to do so.

So, in obedience to God firstly, and secondly at the request of my children and grandchildren, I have recorded these memories of God's influence in my life for posterity.

"Do whatever He tells you" (John 2:5).

CHINA

VISION OF TWO
OPENING DOORS
April 1984

It was the Saturday evening of a weekend conference arranged by the Catholic Bible School and we delegates were happily discussing over supper the various insights gained from the talks given that day.

Despite the babble of conversation, I became aware of one of the convent Sisters, moving from table to table, trying to locate a certain Pauline Doyle. It was my husband, Tom, on the phone.

My heart sank with apprehension at hearing my name, because Tom was supposedly away on a trip. It must be something wrong with one of the children I thought, in growing panic. Happily, this was not the case. Tom had simply arrived home a little earlier than planned and wanted to know if he could join the conference for the remainder of the time.

You cannot know how surprising this was because for the past several years Tom had shown no interest in the prayer group at home, nor indeed Catholic Charismatic Renewal in general.

After a quick discussion with Joan Le Morvan, Head of the Bible School, who was aware of Tom's previous reluctance to join in these events, without hesitation said, "Just tell him to come - we'll sort out his accommodation later!" I didn't realise it then that this event was to put into motion an incredible move of the Holy Spirit in both of our lives.

By the time Tom arrived, supper had finished, and we had all adjourned into the hall, where Ruth Heflin from Jerusalem was ministering. When she prayed with me, I immediately fell under the power of the Holy Spirit and had just fallen to the ground when Tom arrived. I was not aware of Tom, of course, as I lay there, experiencing a most powerful vision and sensation. The vision was of two large doors slightly opened. Above each door was some writing, which I could not understand but I somehow recognised one to be in Chinese and the other in Greek. Meanwhile, the sensation I was experiencing was that of water being poured over my head, as if I were being baptised.

What a shock it must have been for Tom, to see me lying prostrate in this manner, but the fact that he was there, both attending the conference, and especially witnessing this very powerful moment, in some ways made possible what was to follow, in due course.

During the remainder of the conference, Tom became acquainted with Ruth a little more and with her encouragement he even agreed to put our names down for Joan's next pilgrimage to Jerusalem the following year. Without Tom adding our names to the list, I wouldn't have dreamed of doing so because of the considerable cost involved, also because of Tom's hitherto reluctance to become involved with anything 'charismatic.' I jotted down my memories of that day and waited for further revelation, meanwhile taking heed of the following Scripture from Habakkuk:

Write the vision down,
inscribe it on tablets to be easily read.
For the vision is for its appointed time,
it hastens towards its end and it will not lie;
although it may take some time, wait for it,
for come it certainly will before too long.
(NJ Habakkuk. 2:2,3)

THE JOSHUA PROPHECY
June 1984

Since joining Marconi in 1981, I had been part of a Christian Fellowship which met once a week during our lunch break. As frequently happened to me in groups, I found myself the only Catholic, indeed the only woman, which was not so surprising since the company consisted of a largely male workforce.

Involvement with the Christian Fellowship enriched my faith life enormously, as one by one I came to know the individual members and learned to respect their differing beliefs according to their respective denomination. One thing we did appear to have in common was the experience of Baptism in the Holy Spirit and an appreciation of the charismatic gifts of the Holy Spirit.

It was natural, therefore, to bring to the group my recent experience just a few weeks earlier, of the vision given to me, of two opening doors, over which was writing in what appeared to be Chinese and Greek lettering.

Prayer for interpretation followed and unhesitatingly, one of the group, a young man from The Plymouth Brethren Church, responded in prophecy quoting the opening lines of the Book of Joshua (1:1-10). I was not familiar with the passage but remember holding onto the words,

"Every place that the sole of your foot will tread upon I have given to you, as I have given to Moses"
(NRSV Joshua 1:3)

Be strong and courageous; do not be frightened or dismayed, for the Lord your God is with you wherever you go" (NRSV Joshua 1:9)

Again, the group paused to prayerfully 'weigh' this prophecy. After a short time, another member confirmed that the words were for me. To justify his interpretation and conviction, he pointed to his Bible which had been lying open at random since he had placed it down when he first came into the room. It was open at that very passage!

No further elucidation or clarification came on that occasion but a few weeks later these words were prophesied over me once again at the Bible School, by a visiting speaker, and this prophecy would be repeated once more by another complete stranger at a conference. By this time, I knew I was to hold onto God's words until such time as further clarification came.

I did not have to wait long for this to happen. Whilst attending a Retreat at Park Place, the Holy Spirit began to work interiorly upon me, and I became aware of certain promptings. From the very first gathering of the delegates in the chapel, to the final Mass, things began to stir inside.

It was customary on arrival for delegates to assemble in

the chapel. Songs of praise would then flow naturally as a rule. There was no plan - everything was orchestrated by the Holy Spirit moving among us. It was quite natural for someone to begin to sing the first line of a song they felt inspired to sing, then it would be taken up and sung by the rest of the group. This may then be repeated several times until such time as another person was led by the Holy Spirit to pray, prophesy, or start another song. In this way, the service flowed.

Sometimes we would break into singing in tongues. Each person would sing in the 'tongue' or language which they had been given by the Holy Spirit, and the combined sound was as if the angels themselves were singing. Eventually, this would come to a natural close, as if a hidden conductor were conducting. After this, a holy hush would descend and we would pause, alert for a word of Prophecy, which often came after singing in tongues.

At some point, I felt inspired to start the opening lines of a new song we were just learning in the prayer group at home. Still standing, with eyes closed and my heart bursting with great love and fervour, I started to sing spontaneously the following words,

"Here I am, wholly available,
As for me, I will serve the Lord"

Anticipating the other delegates to take up the verses, I waited for a few seconds, but nothing happened. Instead, there was another holy hush. After a few more seconds I instinctively opened my eyes - I did not know the verses anyway and was astonished to find everyone seated. I learned later that as I began to sing, everyone sat down!

It was as if my choice of song was in fact my personal dedication to the Lord. (I learned much later that the song is based on Joshua's declaration in chapter 24, where he swears wholehearted allegiance and faithfulness to the Lord). This too, had been my desire, to make myself 'wholly available' for the Lord's purposes.

As the weekend progressed, I understood, with no little concern, that the Lord's call might necessitate having to leave my employment. This was of considerable concern because without my salary, it would put quite a strain on the family budget, especially providing for two children at university at that time. Nevertheless, this was God's call and I had just pledged wholehearted allegiance. How I would respond would determine whether I follow God's will or my own, whether my response was in fact wholehearted or not.

This was not the first time I had voiced my concerns to the Lord about surrendering my employment, and hadn't He said, in reply,

> *"You know Me as your Lord and Saviour.*
> *You know Me as your Healer.*
> *To know Me more deeply,*
> *You need to know Me as your Provider."*

I had much to consider, prayerfully, for the rest of the retreat, but by the time the concluding Mass came round, my mind was made up; I had made my pledge to be wholly available whatever the cost.

In the final Mass, I was given two visions of Jesus standing at the altar as we approached in line to receive Holy Communion. In the first vision, He appeared to be preparing Bread, the Bread of His Body (John:6) passing the flat unleavened bread from one hand to the other, an inviting expression on His face as we progressed towards Him.

Just as I approached Jesus the vision changed. He was now holding in His hands two golden wedding rings - one for me to take and one for Himself. Through my acceptance, I was now totally consecrated for whatever mission lay ahead.

CALL TO HONG KONG
July/August 1984

It happened as I was taking my coffee break at work one day and reflecting on the report I had just typed, when the words I knew so well by now came drifting into my mind:

"Every place that the sole of your foot will tread upon I have given to you..." (NRSV Joshua 1:3)

At once I was alert, wondering why this quotation should interrupt my present train of thought. A slight shudder passed through my body as I pondered on the possible ramifications of my recent pledge to be wholly available. Within a few seconds, this reverie passed, and I reviewed my next piece of work.

Imperceptibly at first, references to Hong Kong crept to the forefront of my mind; things as obscure as the annual Dragon Boat Race in Hong Kong Harbour, and a popular Christian book called *Chasing the Dragon* about an English missionary living in Hong Kong and doing amazing work with drug addicts in the famous Walled City.

Wherever I looked or whatever I read, Hong Kong, it seemed, caught my attention. Thoughts of Hong Kong persisted over the next few weeks, and I wondered in the end if the Lord was not only catching my attention but in fact calling me there. I dismissed the thought initially since, as we had the privilege of concessionary travel, this would be easy to arrange. To test these promptings, I decided to 'put out a fleece' as Gideon had done before the Lord (Judges 6:33-40) and not to speak about this to anyone, including Tom. Only if Tom mentioned Hong Kong would I give the matter further consideration.

The next event on the calendar was Anne's graduation in a few weeks. For this, I took four days' annual leave to allow a two-night stopover in Manchester.

On my return, I was to receive an incredible shock as I arrived at my office. In fact, two shocks. The filing cabinet had been left flung wide open, files were strewn everywhere, even on the floor, as if burglars had ransacked the place. My chief concern was that some of these may be classified files not returned to Security after their perusal by my boss during my absence.

Just as I was taking in the scene, one of my colleagues rushed in to allay my fears and to explain the blitzed office. In my absence, Marconi had gone through a complete managerial reshuffle, involving a promotion for my boss, to General Manager of another Marconi site. In his haste to leave, he had taken files he might need for his new position, leaving the discarded ones littered everywhere for 'somebody' to clear up.

Realisation dawned on me. As my boss's PA, his departure left me, effectively, without a position. This was my second shock. By their own rulebook, Marconi had not a position of equal status to offer me, leaving the company, and me, in something of a quandary. For several weeks, I checked in each day and had virtually nothing to do and still no position on the horizon.

Was this the cliff-edge I needed, to take the leap of faith and voluntarily offer my resignation? Did God really need to engineer the whole restructuring of Marconi for me to get the point? As I was pondering all of this, the words of the Joshua Prophecy came to mind, again. That was it, I would take the plunge, handing in my notice that very day, without even consulting Tom. It made for a very interesting exchange over dinner that evening, and not the one I had expected.

When I told Tom that I had handed in my notice, much to my surprise, he was delighted, as he now looked forward to our being able to spend more time together between his trips!

"When do you finally leave?" was his only question. I had worked out the date exactly to the day.

"I leave on 7th September."

"Great," he said. "You can accompany me on my trip going out on the 8th."

"Where to?" I queried.

"To Hong Kong."

There it was - Gideon's fleece had worked! I would travel confidently now, in the knowledge that it was, indeed, a calling from the Lord.

Just to complete this part of the story, a few days later,

Tom surprised me with an announcement that since we would no longer have my salary, he had visited the bank and increased my future housekeeping. May I add at this point, too, that Tom had never shown the slightest interest in my salary, yet without ever having discussed my earnings, Tom had actually increased my housekeeping by the exact amount of my salary!

Remember in my chapter entitled *The Joshua Prophecy*, the Lord had said that for me to get to know Him more deeply, I needed to know Him as my Provider? In that moment, I was reassured and knew for certain we could trust Him to provide all our needs in future, as in the promise:

> *"And my God will meet all your needs*
> *according to the riches of His glory*
> *I am going to send you what my Father has*
> *promised in Christ Jesus" (Philippians 4:19).*

During the time I was working out my notice, two interesting scenarios presented themselves. I had mentioned to a friend that I was going with Tom to Hong Kong on one of his trips, but I did not indicate anything other than it being an unexpected treat. He said he knew Jackie Pullinger's sister. Like Jackie, her sister was an Anglican, but her husband was a Catholic, whom I knew vaguely from my own Church, never realising he was related to Jackie by marriage. How interesting, I thought.

The next incident happened at my hairdressers. I had told her about my forthcoming trip, saying nothing of the underlying reason for it. Just then a lady popped her head around the door asking to book an appointment. After my hairdresser tended to her request, she called out to me, "Pauline, this is Jackie Pullinger's sister. Come and meet her. I've just told her about your trip."

It was that chance meeting which gave purpose to my trip to Hong Kong. Jackie, I was told, would be delighted to meet up with anyone from England, especially my having met her sister recently. This would be my calling card and entrance ticket to meet the now famous Jackie Pullinger! In the meantime, I read her book again to be au fait with her work. For the record, I never saw her sister again.

When my notice period was nearly completed, I had a vision during Mass, of a moonlit scene, to the right-hand side of which was the typical Chinese curved roofing on a house, which appeared to be standing in a lake. The building might have been a temple. A full moon was reflecting in the water.

The vision lasted only for a minute but in that glimpse I knew I had seen China. Startled by this, I excitedly shared it with my friend Jenny, who, noted for always having two feet firmly on the ground said, "Well, you are going to Hong Kong, that's near enough!"

I said nothing, but I *knew*.

HARVEST MOON FESTIVAL
10 September 1984

My first sighting of Hong Kong was through the window of the First-Class cabin of a British Airways 747, from which I had a clear view of the tricky manoeuvre the air crew was about to make before landing at Hong Kong International Airport (Kai Tak).

Acknowledged to be the sixth most dangerous airport in the world, I was so glad Tom did not tell me this statistic beforehand. It was technically very demanding because the aircraft could not be flown on instruments, only visually. For the more technically minded, the aircraft had to make a low altitude (below 600 ft) right-hand turn. Prior to this manoeuvre, the aircraft had been heading towards a large red and white checkerboard marker on the mountainside, rather like a dart being aimed at a dartboard. Then came the critical turn.

Sitting on the right-hand side of the cabin, I was even more aware of the acute forty-seven per cent angle, as we all leaned in that direction. Once the turn was completed, I relaxed a little, my emotions changing from apprehension one minute, to relief and immense pride the next, in the knowledge that Tom was operating the aircraft.

In spite of having completed a long flight, Tom was eager to show me some of the sights and to choose where we would dine that evening, so having changed into comfortable clothes, we headed off to the popular Food Street, often frequented by aircrews. Here there was a plethora of restaurants, each displaying menus in their windows.

British Airways 747 making sharp right hand turn coming into Kai Tak airport Hong Kong

For the thousands of foreign visitors to Hong Kong each year and being unfamiliar with the local language, Cantonese, the display food plates in the window had realistic-looking plastic food on them, which gave some indication of what to expect! How I wished they had such visual aids when we visited Japan. On that occasion, I had to take a guess, pointing my finger hopefully at the menu. What eventually turned up was a boiled egg!

By the time we reached Food Street, the light was fading, and I became aware of clusters of children milling around, each bearing aloft a brightly lit lantern. This caught my attention, but I thought no more of it at the time, assuming it to be just a local custom or festival.

I made a good choice of food, which was delicious. Having already made several trips to Hong Kong, Tom's dexterity with chopsticks impressed me enormously, as I struggled to match his skill. It was an interesting evening as I took in all the sights, sounds, smells and customs of this strange environment.

Tom on 747 flight deck

During the evening, we discussed how to make good use of the few days Tom would be with me in Hong Kong, because the crew had to fly to India in the middle of the trip, leaving me in Hong Kong until their return some days later. I had to remain because there had not been sufficient time to arrange for a visa for me before we left England. This would work out perfectly, as it would allow me time to make contact with the only people I knew of in Hong Kong, Jackie Pullinger and Ruth Heflin's Mount Zion Fellowship. I resolved to make contact the very next day.

When I rang Jackie's residence the following morning, the voice of a young Chinese boy answered, only to inform me that Jackie was out of town for a few days on a speaking engagement but would be back just in time to see me before I was due to leave Hong Kong. This, too, turned out to be fortuitous, because Tom was able to join me in what was to be a very eye-opening experience.

I then phoned the Mount Zion Community to see if I could visit them. Initially, that, too, was something of a disappointment, because they asked if I could wait until their Friday evening Prayer Meeting, since the Community spent their days working among the Vietnamese Boat People, refugees from Vietnam.

After some polite conversation, I suppose checking me out a little, Alice, who was leader of the Community, wanted to know how I knew Ruth. Eventually, our conversation became a little more relaxed and it was then that I took the opportunity to enquire about the celebrations I had noticed in the streets the previous evening.

"It's the annual Moon Festival," she said by way of explanation, going on to explain that it was a two-day festival and yesterday (the day we arrived) was the main day, referred to as the Day of the Perfect Moon. With those words, I recalled the vision I had had of the full (perfect) moon and I shared this with Alice, making no mention of China at this point, nor attempting any interpretation.

"Your vision tells me you are here at the right time."

The conversation suddenly changed a gear, to another level. Alice asked if I would care to join the Community on Friday evening and stay for the weekend. This arrangement suited perfectly. It would cover the time Tom was in India and by the time of his return, Jackie would be back for me to visit her.

Having had time to reflect for a moment, Alice asked if I would do them a favour. *What could I possibly do for them?* I thought. Then she explained. The Community had established itself in Hong Kong twenty-five years earlier as a launching pad for missionaries to enter China. Very recently, China had 'opened the door' slightly, not necessarily for missionaries but for Westerners in general. Seizing the opportunity, the Community had been taking advantage of this opening up, sending one of their members, a young Australian girl called Jeanette, into China each weekend with a hidden supply of bibles. Alice then asked if I would be prepared to join Jeanette, hoping that two Westerners might pass for mere tourists, and not attract too much attention.

Alice was convinced that the vision given to me was prophetic and with this piece of information, felt it was all in God's plan.

Having agreed to Alice's invitation to attend their Friday Prayer Meeting and to travel to Canton the following day, she asked if I would go into Kowloon in the meantime, to apply for a permit and to purchase a one-way ticket to Canton, today known as Guangzhou. Only one-way tickets were issued at that time, and you had to apply for a return one on the other side!

In the meantime, Tom and I enjoyed the sights of Hong Kong, taking the Hong Kong Victoria Peak Tram on our first day of sight-seeing. The Peak Tram is not really a tram but a cable-hauled funicular railway, which has been scaling the 394 metres (1292 feet 8 inches) ascent to the highest point on Hong Kong Island since 1888.

Once at the Peak, there were magnificent views over the harbour and soaring skyscrapers. There was also a small gift shop, from which I purchased a very typical Chinese artwork of cherry blossom painted onto a cork surface. The painting, about 4 feet wide and 2 feet deep, folds by means of four hinged sections, so was easily accommodated in my suitcase.

Two more days followed before Tom would be going to India, which we crammed to the full, closing the last evening with a visit to the famous Jumbo Floating Restaurant in a fishing village in Aberdeen. Another local custom awakened my senses to the differences between Chinese and English sensibilities. Customers in the Jumbo Restaurant could choose a fish from a large fish tank inside and before you knew it, it was on the customer's plate!

The next day the crew was about to depart for India, and I had decided to travel to Kowloon on the Star Ferry to obtain the permit to enter China, along with a one-way ticket to Canton. Meanwhile, on their way to the airport, the captain enquired how I was planning to fill my time while they were away. He was absolutely horrified when Tom told him of my plans.

"Surely, you're not going to let her do that are you?" he enquired.

In reply, Tom simply said, "She will be okay, she's in God's hands."

Moments like this were infrequent, but on occasion Tom had been similarly reassured by the Holy Spirit on my behalf.

Despite my inability to understand the language and currency, or to read timetables, I surprised myself by accomplishing all I had set out to do. At the station, the queue for tickets and permits had been long, as people eagerly strained to get their first glimpse of mainland China. It all certainly took me well out of my comfort zone, I assure you! Now I had to make the journey in reverse.

It happened in the middle of Hong Kong Harbour, taking me completely by surprise; a sudden sensation as if warm oil were being trickled over my head, the warmth eventually covering my whole body. It remained with me for several minutes and then it was gone, just as quickly as it had come. I recognised this to be an anointing by the Holy Spirit, in preparation for the forthcoming mission to China. In two days' time, I would learn more about my involvement when I joined the Community on Friday evening for their Prayer Meeting.

Back at the hotel, I again caught up with my daily readings, which I had not completed in the morning. I gained further insight from the Gospel reading, words which would impress themselves all the more, in view of the experience I had had on my return trip on the Star Ferry:

"I am going to send you what your Father has promised;
*but **stay in the city** until you have been clothed with*
power from on high" (Luke 24:49)

The opened door to China now awaited me.

THE DOOR TO CHINA OPENS
September 1984

Friday evening came at last, and I was collected by Alice to join the Community's Prayer Meeting. Despite having worked tirelessly all week with the Vietnamese refugees, their enthusiastic praise was not diminished at all. It was a wonderful time of free-flowing praise and worship, lasting for quite some time.

After a while, and taking me quite by surprise, I was introduced to the Community and called upon to share what had brought me there. I spoke about the Joshua Prophecy, with the specific words:

"Every place that the sole of your foot will tread upon I have given to you..."(NRSV Joshua 1:3)

I went on to explain how this had led to a call to Hong Kong, via a vision of a full or 'Perfect' moon.

Alice took up the story at this point, highlighting the significance of the vision and the accurate timing of my arrival in Hong Kong, on the main day of the Harvest Moon Festival, the Day of the Perfect Moon.

Susan, a co-leader with Alice, was then called upon to

speak about her specific calling. Hearing her testimony made mine feel a little less obscure and mysterious, but first a little background to Susan is appropriate and may be of interest.

Before Susan joined the Community, she was an archaeologist. At some point, she had a powerful conversion experience, was baptised in the Holy Spirit, and gave up her job as an archaeologist to join the Community. She spent several years in Jerusalem as co-Associate with Ruth Heflin, but recently, since the door to China was beginning to open, she had received a new commission.

Looking at me she said, "If you think your commission seems strange, just wait till you hear mine." As mine was to walk, claiming the land; the Lord had requested that she climb all the sacred mountains in China and claim them for the Lord. No mean task!

After the meeting, I was taken aside and given some details about my forthcoming trip to Canton with one of Alice's colleagues, Jeanette. The brief information I was given was that we would each be carrying a holdall containing thirty bibles, which would be deposited in the left luggage department of the hotel where we were to stay overnight. These would eventually be collected by Christian missionaries for use with potential converts.

The following morning my newfound colleague and I made our way across the harbour on the Star Ferry to Kowloon, where we joined the queue for the train. Although packed with people, the atmosphere in the train was surprisingly quiet, with people speaking in subdued whispers. We followed suit, hardly passing a word between us, except to point out, surreptitiously, several other passengers sitting adjacent to us. They, too, were on the same mission as we, smuggling bibles.

The journey from Kowloon to Canton, a mere 131 Km (81 miles) seemed endless, with such a sombre atmosphere and very little conversation. After travelling for an hour or so, Jeanette made me aware of the possible danger we were risking by taking bibles into China. There would be serious consequences for us if we were identified by the patrolling authorities at our train destination. My instructions were, once at the station, I was to keep quite separate from her in the hope that if she were to be singled out for inspection, I could walk on unnoticed. As it happened, neither of us was checked and we met up again at the end of the station approach. This opened out to a very wide road, which we crossed and made our way to a nearby hotel. There we lodged our holdalls in the left luggage, checked in at Reception and made our way to our room. Only then did I realise that if Jeanette had been intercepted, I did not know where I was supposed to go! With a sigh of relief, I stretched out on the bed to wait for dinner. Mission accomplished, I thought, as I reflected on what may have happened.

The next morning Jeanette informed me that we had another little mission in Canton itself before returning to Kowloon later that day. This brings me back to Susan's mission to climb all the sacred mountains in China. As already mentioned, she had previously been an archaeologist and because of this interest she brought back a specimen of rock as a memento from each of the mountains that she scaled. These she displayed on wooden mounts, uniquely carved to accommodate each rock shape. Our mission was to visit a furniture maker, who specialised in ornate Chinese woodcarving whom she had found to carve the mounts.

Moving through the streets towards the bus stop, I became aware of the stares we were attracting from everyone. It was obvious the people were unfamiliar with the sight of Westerners. The degree of curiosity we attracted was all the more apparent once we were aboard the bus. Shared giggles and stares were focussed directly on us throughout our journey. The intense interest was not just because of our large stature in comparison to most of the local people, but also because of the shape of our nose! The Westerners were known colloquially as 'big noses.'

The second stage of our journey was undertaken by means of a ride in a two-seater motorised rickshaw, which was able to wind its way more deftly through the narrow streets.

Once at the furniture manufacturer's premises, we were shown into a waiting room by a young girl of about eighteen, who spoke English. We would have to wait some time for the owner of the business to see us; in the meantime, she offered a refreshing drink of green tea, obviously eager to practice her English while we waited.

Eventually, the owner of the business came, holding Susan's mounts in his hands. While he was momentarily occupied with paperwork, Jeanette whispered to me that there was a problem. It was obvious to her, even from a cursory glance, that the mounts were not satisfactory for some reason, which posed another, even greater problem. Pointing out his mistake would mean he would lose face, which to the Chinese is tantamount to an insult! There was only one thing she could do - pass more pleasantries and make many compliments about other artefacts which were on show, before finally adding the inevitable 'but.' Many cups of green tea were drunk as these pleasantries were exchanged, which not only gave the translator an opportunity to develop her language skill but afforded a chance to engage with her at a deeper level.

The compliments worked and eventually it was possible to explain how his work was not quite what had been expected. After yet more green tea, the owner acknowledged his mistake and promised to have replacement mounts ready by her next visit to Canton.

Eventually, it was time to leave, and the owner asked the interpreter to escort us to the rickshaw pickup area. In doing this, we passed through many grimy narrow streets, so narrow it was impossible for the three of us to walk alongside each other, forcing me to drop behind them.

Feeling somewhat left out of their exchanges, I grumbled a little to myself. It was then that the Lord spoke to me saying, "You came here to walk, not talk!'

Once again, the words came as if to remind me.

*"Every place that the sole of your foot will tread upon
I have given to you..."(NRSV Joshua 1:3)*

Eventually, we arrived at the rickshaw pickup place and

made our way back to the hotel. The rest of our time was uneventful and the following day, we made the return train ride to Kowloon without any difficulties arising. There, we said our farewells and I made my way back to Hong Kong Island via the Star Ferry. In a few hours' time, Tom and the crew would be back from India, and we could take up Jackie Pullinger's invitation to lunch the following day.

MEETING WITH
JACKIE PULLINGER
HONG KONG
September 1984

The year 1966 was memorable for many reasons. It was the year the England football team won the World Cup; for me, it commemorated the birth of my third child, Peter; but for one seemingly insignificant yet plucky young woman from England, it was to herald the beginning of a remarkable career. One day she would be honoured in her country of origin with an MBE, and an Honorary degree of Doctor of Social Sciences (HKG), for her dedication and incredible success in treating drug addicts in the infamous Walled City in Kowloon.

These honours had yet to be bestowed upon Jackie Pullinger when I met her in 1984, but I had become aware of her work through her book *Chasing the Dragon*, first printed in 1980, and on its third printing in 1983, when I purchased a copy.

This luncheon opportunity had come about through the chance meeting with her sister at my hairdressers, as I recalled earlier.

The Walled City (the name means 'darkness' in Chinese) was a lawless slum, full of opium dens, pornographic film theatres, gambling dens and triad gangs, who profited from crime and prostitution. All kinds of illegal buildings had gone up because they did not need building permission. They were like card houses, often built one on top of another. No daylight penetrated the city; there was no running water, electricity, or sanitation. It was said that there were more rats than the estimated 100,000 people. There were only two toilets at the entrance, one for women, one for men.

Jackie had toiled tirelessly in the Walled City, responding to needs as best she could, but the people did not usually want to hear about Jesus. All this changed, however, when she received the charismatic 'Gift of Tongues' just as the Apostles had at Pentecost (Acts 2). Praying in this way, her ministry to the addicts changed dramatically. When she took this gift into her prayer life and work, God honoured her efforts. As she set to work loving the unlovable, former heroin addicts found themselves miraculously healed from their addictions, and they, too, prayed in tongues. Crime bosses surrendered their lives to Jesus and prostitutes quit their profession.

It soon became apparent that these former addicts needed a period of rehabilitation, to learn more about their new faith. They also needed a period of readjustment to normal life. Their bodies were healed from addiction, but they needed ordinary socialisation, because they knew no other form of living but to steal. Eventually, what we might call 'rehab houses' were set up for this purpose, and addicts would stay in these homes for a minimum of a year, ideally for two.

It was to one of these rehab houses that Tom and I were invited to join Jackie over lunch. What remains with me to this day is the incredible atmosphere of peace and joy which pervaded the humble setting. Just like a large family sitting around the dining room table, Jackie and her 'boys' as she called them, invited Tom and me to join them. Like any group of people, there were extroverts who were quite willing to relate their conversion stories, whilst others listened shyly, beaming, and nodding in recognition, as the storyteller recalled their common experience.

All too quickly, it was time for us to leave, and Jackie asked one of the boys, called Luke, to escort us to the bus stop. It was unbelievable to think that these boys had once been guilty of heinous crimes yet were now so obviously transformed. It had been an honour and a privilege to have been invited into their lives, albeit for a short time.

Jackie takes no glory in the telling of her success. Her legacy, if she has one, is that the people she led to Christ can and do, in their turn, lead others to new life and true freedom in Christ.

> *"I have come that they might have life,*
> *and have it to the full." (John 10:10)*

FULFILMENT IN JERUSALEM
March 1985

It was Spring 1985, and Tom and I had the privilege of making a pilgrimage to the Holy Land with the Catholic Bible School.

You may recall that Tom had placed our names down for this pilgrimage, at the invitation of Ruth Heflin. She promised we would be greatly blessed, and it was certainly turning out to be the pilgrimage of a lifetime, in so many ways.

We had travelled to Tel Aviv apart from the rest of the group, using our concessionary travel permit, planning to meet up later with them, in Nazareth.

After a long bus ride from the airport at Tel Aviv, we finally arrived in Nazareth. Everything was strange, as we looked around on alighting from the bus. My attention was suddenly attracted by the voice of a little boy, calling for his father. Although it was not my language, he was calling out using the only word in Hebrew which I knew – "Abba" (Daddy). It is the intimate term used by a child to its father, and the name which Jesus used in teaching His followers how to address God, His Father, in prayer. It is the name that I had become used to using in prayer myself, ever since my Baptism in the Holy Spirit, when I really came to know God as my Father!

The scene changed, and yet another biblical expression was to come alive before our eyes. Having arrived safely in Nazareth, we needed to know how to get to our rendezvous with the Bible School group. Approaching the first person we saw who we thought might speak English, we asked for directions to the site of the House of the Holy Family, expecting him to give verbal instructions. Instead, pointing to his chest, he said, "I am the way," and beckoned for us to follow him!

True to his word, he was indeed 'the way,' as he led us through the twists and turns of many narrow streets and passageways. Finally coming to a halt, face beaming with pleasure, he indicated that we had arrived; he had brought us safely to our destination.

This experience illustrated beautifully for us the words of Jesus' saying, "I am the Way." It was so clear now. Jesus Himself would lead us to our final destination (heaven) if we trusted Him and followed Him, just as we had trusted this complete stranger. Interestingly, the early Christians were known as 'The People of the Way,' alluding to the way they lived their lives.

As interesting and illuminating as these simple teaching moments were, by far the greatest revelation also occurred in Nazareth, when we celebrated Mass in the Church of the Annunciation on the Feast of St Joseph.

Before heading south, we made a quick visit to Cana,

eight miles away, the site of the Wedding Feast where Jesus performed His first miracle, in changing water into wine. (John 2:1-12).

Taking in as many biblical sites as we could, as we made our way to our ultimate destination, Jerusalem, our next place of interest was to the River Jordan, where baptisms were likely to have taken place at the time of Jesus. There, standing in the river, we renewed our Baptismal vows, reflecting as we did so, on the story of John the Baptist's ministry and the baptism of Jesus Himself (Matthew 3:13-17).

Continuing our pilgrimage, we made our way to Lake Galilee. Traditionally called the Sea of Galilee, it is in fact a lake, 53 km (33 miles) long and 21km (13 miles wide). At 209 metres (686 feet) below sea level, it is the lowest freshwater lake on Earth and the second lowest after the Dead Sea, which is a saltwater lake. Along the shoreline, we visualised the calling of the first disciples (Matthew 4:18-22).

At Capernaum, where Jesus based His ministry, we recalled the long discourse of Jesus, and His astonishing claim, *"I AM the Bread of Life" (John 6:22-59)*. There, we saw the remains of Peter's house and recalled how Jesus cured Peter's mother-in-law from a fever (Matthew 8:14-15).

Nearby, we visited the site of The Sermon on the Mount, a collection of Jesus' moral teachings to guide His disciples, based on the new law of love, even of enemies, as opposed to the Old Testament law of retribution, 'an eye for an eye, a tooth for a tooth.' This sermon is one of five discourses in Matthew's gospel, which includes The Beatitudes and

The Lord's Prayer recorded in Matthew chapters 5, 6 and 7.

A little further along the shore of the Sea of Galilee, we visited a small church at Tabgah, in which there were the remains of a mosaic floor depicting the miracle of the feeding of the five thousand, from five loaves and two fish. The church was said to mark the spot where this miracle occurred. There, we celebrated Mass just before lunch.

I had always wondered how a crowd as large as five thousand people could hear Jesus' preaching, but the first disciples, fishermen, had long since learned the skill of calling out to each other across the water, knowing from experience that the sound would be amplified by the water. We are told that Jesus had His companions pull out a few yards from the shoreline, and standing up in the boat, He projected his voice across the water. In this manner, He could be heard by the crowds.

Little anecdotes such as this brought the scripture passages to life and made them more believable to the sceptic.

As we travelled into lower Galilee, we saw from a distance Mount Tabor at the eastern end of the Jezreel Valley, eleven miles west of the Sea of Galilee. The highest point of Mount Tabor is referenced as the place of the Transfiguration. In the account, Jesus took with Him Peter, James and John. Once on the mountain, Matthew states that Jesus was 'transfigured' before them; His face shining as the sun, and His garments became white as the light (Matthew 17:2-3).

At that point, Moses, representing the Law, and Elijah, representing the Prophets, appeared, and Jesus began to talk to them. The three disciples then heard a voice from heaven saying, *"This my Son, whom I have chosen; Listen to Him." (Luke 9:35).*

Having been shown in His glory, Jesus is now affirmed by His Father and the fact that they are told to "listen to Him" indicates that Jesus' teaching is greater than that which has gone before. The Transfiguration is a sign that Jesus was to fulfil the Law and the Prophets and that He was indeed the Messiah.

For two further days, we were housed in a small cottage at the lakeside. Stepping from the door, we were immediately walking on the shingle leading down to the water's edge. From there, we could see fishing boats bobbing up and down, as they cast their nets, just as they had fished for hundreds of years, before and since the time of Jesus.

At the time of Jesus, there were an estimated 230 fishing boats fishing in this sea of plenty.

Another 'Sea' we visited was the Dead Sea. Again, it is technically another lake, but unlike the Sea of Galilee, there is no life in it because of the salt, but it did make for an entertaining afternoon floating in its waters.

To the west of the Dead Sea is located Qumran, the site where the Dead Sea Scrolls were discovered in eleven caves, between 1947 and 1966. This is the area where the Essenes, a strict Jewish sect, said to have been preparing for the imminent coming of the Messiah, lived and practised their beliefs. It is thought that John the Baptist may have been one of their adherents.

Eventually, we reached Jericho, the lowest place on Earth.

It is a delightful oasis, and place of probably the most famous parable in the New Testament, The Good Samaritan, (Luke 10:25-37) covering Jesus' main moral teaching, that we should show love and compassion to everyone, including our enemies.

Historically, Samaritans were despised by Jews because they had 'contaminated' the purity of the Jewish Faith through inter-marriage during the time of the Babylonian Exile. By the time of Jesus, they had become a despised sect and were thought of as enemies. According to Jesus, love for one's neighbour (including Samaritans) should come before rules, even religious rules, which the priest and Levite were most concerned with, as they passed by the injured man in the parable. (According to Jewish teaching, one could be defiled if one touched a dead body, and the injured man might have been dead).

It took a Samaritan, one of a despised sect of Jews, to show compassion and mercy to the man left for dead on the roadside. (A demonstration of Jesus' new law of love for everyone). A salutary lesson for us all!

The story of Zacchaeus, a chief tax collector for the vicinity of Jericho and employed by the Roman Empire, occurred in Jericho. Jesus was passing through and crowds had come out to see Him, among them Zacchaeus. We are told in the Gospel account that Zacchaeus, being a short man, had climbed a sycamore tree to see Jesus. According to reputation, it seems more likely that he did not wish to be seen because of his unpopularity. (Firstly, he was a Jew, employed by the Roman Empire, paid to extract taxes from his own people, the Jews. Secondly, they were often corrupt, overtaxing the people).

As the story unfolds, Jesus notices Zacchaeus and calls him down, asking if He might dine with him that evening. As a result of this encounter, Zacchaeus is converted, promising to pay back up to four times the amount he had over-taxed (Luke 19:1-10).

In Tiberius, we were taken right out to the middle of the Sea of Galilee in a large boat. Although it was a fine day, we read the account of the miracle of the calming of the storm (Matthew 8:23-27). On that beautiful balmy day, it was difficult to imagine a violent storm suddenly occurring, but we were assured by our guide that because of its low-lying position in the Rift Valley and surrounded by hills, the sea can suddenly get violent, and a storm whipped up in a matter of minutes.

After the boat trip, we had lunch in a restaurant alongside the lake. On the menu, there was a fish called 'St Peter's Fish.' For explanation, we were referred to the story where the disciples had no coin with which to pay the Temple Tax. On Jesus' instruction, St Peter caught a fish and found in its mouth the exact coin with which to pay the tax (Matthew 17:24-27).

To this day, a certain fish bearing what appears to be the marks of a person's thumb and forefinger, is still fished there; a fish which has the habit of swallowing coin-size objects, which get stuck in its throat. These days one is not likely to find a Temple Tax coin, but many Coca-Cola bottle tops are commonly found in its throat!

The miracle of the coin in the mouth of the fish is true; the story of the finger and thumb marks may be an elaboration. Fact or tradition, it made for an interesting conversation over lunch.

Another detour took us to Sychar, where we visited Jacob's Well where Jesus had the encounter with the Samaritan woman (John 4: 4-42). I am particularly fond of this passage, for reasons shared elsewhere, so I will not repeat it here.

Biblical scenes were brought to life when we spent two days at the Biblical Institute in Tantur, just a few miles from Jerusalem. There we spent the mornings in class studying various parables and especially some of the "I AM" sayings of Jesus, such as

> *"I AM the Good Shepherd," (John 10:11),*
> *"I AM the Vine," (John: 15:5) and*
> *"I AM the gate," (John 10:7).*

After lunch each day, we were taken on field trips, scrambling into a small bus, and transported to various agricultural settings and scenes. Here we were shown vines, wine presses, fig trees, millstones and sheepfolds, all of which Jesus had used as visual aids when teaching His disciples.

In one section of the grounds of the Institute, a watchtower had been erected. In another area, a sheepfold had been built, with its thorny briars firmly fixed on top of the stone-walled pen built by the shepherd for safe night shelter, and to deter wolves.

There was only one way to enter the sheepfold, and this was where the shepherd laid himself across the opening, to defend the sheep, in the likelihood of a wolf daring to slip in. The 'Good' Shepherd is the one who literally lays down his life for the sheep (as Jesus would do on the cross).

'Very truly, I tell you, I am the gate for the sheep.'
(John 10:7)

It was difficult to leave Tantur after two days of stimulating bible study and field trips, but we had to press on. As we reached the outskirts of Bethlehem, which we learned means 'House of Bread' another I AM saying immediately sprang to mind, when Jesus, speaking of Himself, spoke the words, "I AM the Bread of Life." Jesus referred to Himself thus in the long discourse found in John 6:22-59, preached in the synagogue in Capernaum.

Another interesting fact I did not know about Bethlehem, apart from being the birthplace of Jesus, is that all the lambs which were to be sacrificed at Passover time were reared in the hills around Bethlehem, and the little lambs, a week or so before Passover, had to walk the seven miles to Jerusalem, to be led to their sacrificial slaughter. Likewise, Jesus, the true Passover Lamb, would walk to Jerusalem to His sacrificial death. Even the time recorded in the Gospels of the hour of His death concurred with the time the lambs were slaughtered (the ninth hour or 3 pm). Parallels such as this were springing up everywhere.

A few miles outside of Jerusalem, we passed through Bethany, a traditional spot of pilgrimage on the slopes of the Mount of Olives, some one and a half miles east of Jerusalem. There, we visited the traditional site of the tomb of Lazarus, pausing to meditate on the final and most profound I AM saying of Jesus –

"I AM the Resurrection and the Life" (John 11:25)

spoken in the Raising of Lazarus from the dead.

The account of the raising of Lazarus is one of the most moving episodes recorded in the life of Jesus. Lazarus, along with his sisters, Martha and Mary, was a very dear friend and we are told that Jesus 'wept over Lazarus,' not so much that he had died, for He knew the miracle that He was about to perform, but because of the power of death over all mankind.

Jerusalem was now in sight, and when we reached our destination, we traced the final steps of Jesus in His last week. Before that, I tried to visualise the scene. It was Passover time, the population of Jerusalem would have swelled to an estimated two million Jews from all over the known world, having made one of the three mandatory pilgrimages to the Holy City. The lambs, one for each family according to custom, had spent the previous five days with their designated 'family.' Now, the bleating of the estimated 600,000 lambs, which would be slaughtered at Passover, filled the air.

The night before Jesus' death, He had requested His disciples to prepare a room to celebrate Passover. We call this place The Upper Room, where Jesus would perform His last and greatest miracle, in leaving us His Body and Blood to sustain us on our journey through life.

The exact site of the Upper Room is not known but there is a room where this occasion has been commemorated since the Middle Ages. At this site, we visualised the disciples preparing for the traditional meal and indeed the meal itself. At Tantur, life-size models seated around a typical celebratory Passover Meal, had formed a completely different image in our minds from the familiar paintings of the Last Supper. At Tantur, we were also guided through the proceedings of a typical Passover Meal, or Seder, and these images came to mind at this time.

Next, we visited The Garden of Gethsemane (Matthew 26:36-56) on the Mount of Olives, where Jesus experienced such agony at the thought of what lay before Him the next day, it is recorded that He sweat blood.

You may ask, is this possible? For centuries, believers have faithfully believed the Scriptural account. Today, we no longer have to exercise faith to believe; science can now prove the veracity of the Gospel account, with its advanced scientific knowledge. This phenomenon can be explained. The condition is called HEMATOHIDROSIS, a rare clinical phenomenon. It is a condition in which the capillary blood vessels that feed the sweat glands rupture, causing them to exude blood, occurring under conditions of extreme physical or emotional stress. I would add, too, sheer terror.

We see, in this episode, the real humanity of Jesus. Although He was both human and divine, He did not shy away from the real pain and suffering that He would endure the following day.

It is difficult to visualise Mount Calvary as it was at the time of Jesus' death, because the spot has been marked over the centuries with churches built to commemorate the exact place of Jesus' sacrificial death. The Church of the Holy Sepulchre, the site of Calvary, the tomb of Jesus, and the place of the Resurrection, is the holiest place in the Christian world.

We had our customary Mass celebrated right there, at Calvary, using the Mass set we had bought in the local shops, on which was depicted the mosaic of the feeding of the five thousand, mentioned earlier when we visited Tabgah.

We stayed in Jerusalem for several days, allowing time to revisit the memorable sites. We became quite familiar with following the Via Dolorosa (the way of sorrows or suffering), the route through the old city of Jerusalem commemorating the path Jesus took on His way to His crucifixion. There are fourteen stopping points or 'stations' along the Via Dolorosa, where appropriate Scriptures are reflected upon.

At a point in history when Christians were no longer able to visit the Holy Land on pilgrimage, the practice of establishing pictures or carvings of the scenes represented, were set up in all Catholic Churches throughout the world. The devotion is still in common practice, especially during Lent and all Fridays. The prayers can also be said privately in the home.

With one day left before our departure, we had an unexpected surprise when we visited Ruth Heflin. (This was at the invitation of Ruth last year at the Bible School Conference).

Ruth was hosting a Conference in Jerusalem that day, arranged by the Community. She was already on stage when we caught up with her, as she welcomed people from different parts of the world. They were coming up to her in small, representative groups, where Ruth engaged them in conversation about what had brought them to Jerusalem.

Several groups had already presented themselves, when suddenly there was Alice from Hong Kong, guiding a small group of people! As she came up to the microphone, she was so obviously delighted to tell their story for them, because their English was very limited.

It was a thrill and surprise for me, too, to see Alice again, but that paled into insignificance when I subsequently heard their story!

As mentioned previously, Mount Zion Fellowship in Hong Kong had been established as a springboard into China, for whenever the door to China was opened. That time had now arrived, and Alice went on to tell the story of their first converts to Christianity. Incredibly, the very first convert turned out to be the young interpreter who I had met in Canton when I travelled there by train with the young Australian missionary, Jeanette. Soon after the young interpreter's conversion, her whole family followed suit, along with many others.

Alice described this remarkable story as "The Door to China has now opened!" What a fulfilling ending to our amazing pilgrimage!

With the information about the first Chinese converts, the words of the wine steward at the Wedding Feast at Cana came to me,

> *"You have saved the best wine till now."*
> *(John 2:10).*

CHALLENGES AND
BLESSINGS

THE HARDEST CHOICE
15 January 1985

The earliest memory I have is of my father taking me to a shallow lake to sail a small boat, which he had bought for me. It was one of my happiest memories but also one of my most frightening. I was aged about three or four at the time.

I had gently pushed the small boat away from the lakeside and was following its movement through the water when, turning back to where my father was standing, in order to share this momentary pleasure, I suddenly realised he had gone.

Sheer panic flooded through my mind for a few moments, and then I heard his reassuring voice calling me, and all was well again. What my childish brain had not comprehended was that he had not moved from where I had left him. It was I who had moved, following the trajectory of the boat. Is that not just the same in the spiritual life? We can sometimes feel God has left us or has distanced Himself from us. Yet the reality is that it is we who have moved away from God the Father, whilst He stays constant. This first memory has stayed with me all of my life and the spiritual truth contained therein reinforces my belief in the faithfulness and dependability of my Heavenly Father.

I adored my father. He was my hero. Physically strong and tall, at just over six feet, his physicality belied his kind and gentle nature. I have many happy memories of listening out for 'our' whistle in the early evening, heralding his approach at the end of our street. I would respond immediately, rushing towards his outstretched arms, when he would swing me round and round, to my sheer delight. Sometimes, he would carry me aloft in his arms, but as I grew older, I walked proudly alongside him, hand in hand, as we strode the rest of the way together.

Other memories I recall were moments shared in the mornings. Houses were very cold in those days, but my father always lit a fire before waking up the rest of the family. He knew I loved these special moments in his company, so would wrap me up in the bundle of still warm blankets and place me on the settee, where I could see him lighting the fire. It was worth being cold for a time until the fire got going but every moment spent with him was precious. This was especially true, because these were post-war days and my father, who worked in the building trade as a concreter, worked on various building sites around the country, often necessitating his having to work away from home from Monday to Friday. At other times, when the site was some distance away, he would even have to work away for several weeks.

As I grew a little older, he spent a few minutes each morning teaching me how to tell the time and how to read, with the result that I was a pre-school reader! Amazing to think of that, for there were no special teaching aids in those days and he did not teach me phonetically and the letters were all in capitals.

At the end of the working day, after I had answered 'our' whistle and we had arrived home together, he was confronted with the draughts board, already lined up for a challenging game later in the evening. Awaiting, too, were his slippers warming in the hearth. Mum always emphasised how important that was, after he had spent all day in the cold. But first there was his usual ritual of greeting with a kiss, first my mother, my young brother, David, and myself, after which he would remove his soiled working clothes before washing his hands at the kitchen sink. Funny how taste and smell are such evocative trigger senses. I can still smell that distinctive smell of concrete on his overalls, which I instantly associate with him.

Ritual complete, we would sit down at the table. Once seated, he would go round the table asking each of us in turn, starting with my mother, how our day had gone. Each account was listened to respectfully. My mother may only have visited the butchers and bought sausages or perhaps mince for the meal, yet the telling of it was treated with the utmost respect and interest.

He was an engaging storyteller. His stories emanating from his own lived experience. For instance, the time he swam between Liverpool, his hometown, and New Brighton, a distance of approximately four miles. Yes, this is a true story and verified by my three aunties, his sisters!

On another occasion, at the age of thirteen, he ditched

into the Mersey a handcart full of groceries, which he was delivering in the dock area, in order to answer the call from a fishing boat captain looking for a cabin boy. With only minutes to decide, he ditched the handcart and jumped aboard the vessel, which was just setting out to fish around Iceland. They were away from the home port for three weeks. From this adventure, he developed a great love for the sea. Years later, he became a deep-sea fisherman and followed this career for ten years, providing lots of material for stories in the future! Incidentally, the handcart and load of groceries were found in the Mersey, and it was presumed he had drowned. When he returned to Liverpool, flush with the money he had earned, he could not wait to hand this over to his mother to alleviate the domestic poverty. Instead of gratitude, his father gave him the hiding of a lifetime for causing the family such anguish, the more so as he was the only surviving boy in the family. (Joseph, twin brother of Mary (Molly) had died at three weeks old, and James had choked to death at the age of three.)

Apart from real life stories, drawn from lived experiences, there were endless stories from his lively imagination, no doubt inspired by his days as a deep-sea fisherman. Of special memory, were the stories of the fictitious 'Oodlum' bird, so named because of its call, "Oodlum, Oodlum, Oodlum." Bedtime, therefore, was always something to look forward to, and I hung on his every word!

On one occasion, my teacher asked each of us to find out what our fathers did in the war. My father did not go to war because his type of work, in the building trade, was classified as reserved employment.

Coming from Liverpool, and having a great sense of humour, in answer to my question, "What did you do in the war, Daddy?" he told me he was "in the Fireside Lancers" which sounded very impressive to my young ears. Translated from Liverpool-speak, this meant that he sat by the fire and stoked it up! (The poker was his lance.) Not understanding his reply, I naively took this answer into school and can only now imagine the laugh it raised in the staff room!

Another fireside image comes to mind as I write these reminiscences. As I recall, Mum would be sitting on the left-hand side of the fireplace, usually knitting, listening to the radio (no TV in those days) whilst Dad was on the right-hand side absorbed in some book or other, either a good 'cowie' as he called a Western, or some deep-sea adventure. I even remember the author of the many cowboy books he read. The author was Zane Gray.

And where were David and I in this scene? David, being seven years younger, would either have been in bed already, or in later years, entertaining himself with his pet animals, or conducting chemical experiments in the kitchen, whilst I would be sitting on the settee doing my homework. What I especially recall about this homely scene, was that no matter how absorbed in a book my father was, he was somehow always alert to being called to "make a brew" or, in later years, when Mum became disabled, to respond to whatever her need was at the moment. Always it was carried out with kindness, good humour, and patience.

On one occasion, when my father was working away from

home, I could not understand the concern and apprehension which filled my mind on his behalf. I was old enough not to mention my concern to my mother, which would have set her into a panic, because she was very anxious by nature, so I kept it to myself all week long.

Saturday came and I was waiting for the usual whistle signalling his return. When finally, I heard it, I ran towards him in my usual manner, but there was no sweeping me up into his arms that day, for one of his feet was very heavily bandaged and he was limping badly. Later, we learned there had been an accident on the building site and a huge steel girder had fallen across his toes, causing serious injury. Immediately, I knew that this was what I had been alerted to during the week. I did not realise it at the time, but this was a prompting of the Holy Spirit, changing my concern into prayer for him.

Our relationship developed and during my teen years, to my delight, Dad returned to the practice of his Catholic faith, and we used to walk to Mass together each Sunday. He always made any outing a pleasurable experience and this was no exception. On the way home from church, we would call in at Sivouri's ice cream parlour to savour the various flavours. Yes, those were the days when, apart from at the seaside, you only ate indoors, especially ice cream! In the summer we ate ice cream and in the colder months we drank a glass of hot Vimto.

After this, we usually parted company, while Dad, who had bought a newspaper by this time, branched off from me to go to the Palm Court Hotel, a pub attached to the Belle

Vue Zoo and Entertainment Complex, for a relaxing pint and a read, returning later, when the customary Sunday roast would be ready.

The day I married, he was the proudest of fathers, just as he had been at my birth, so I am told. Our affection for each other was sustained throughout the years and I was pleased to share him with my own children, who in turn thought the world of him, too. Indeed, daughter

Pauline with her proud father 1961

Anne's choice of Manchester university was greatly influenced by the knowledge that she could visit Grandad and the rest of the family, for we had moved south by that time.

It was customary for Grandad to visit in the summer and again at Christmas. What turned out to be his last Christmas, he declined all our offers to pick him up from Manchester and bring him to us for the holiday, saying he was feeling a bit 'off,' with a chesty cough. Perhaps we should have realised it was more than just a chesty cough, knowing how much he looked forward to spending time with us, but since he had suffered from emphysema all his life, which was not helped by his heavy smoking, we just reluctantly had to accept his decision not to join us.

Once again, I was alerted to there being something

wrong, just as I had been when he had had the accident on the site. It was the morning of 15th January when I became aware of some disquiet within me. As it continued, I decided to put aside what I was doing and picked up my Bible, instinctively opening it up at the Psalms. After reading one or two, my eyes fell on Psalm 51, which I prayed, not knowing why I had been drawn to this particular one.

Later that day, news of my father's death reached us from Manchester, and I knew then the reason for the morning's disquiet. It was confirmed that night when Tom suggested, just before retiring for the night, that we should read the Prayers for the Dead. There, the prayers centred around Psalm 51! I can never know for sure, but in my heart, I feel that my dad died or was dying at the moment I was praying Psalm 51.

I immediately telephoned my brother to pass on the sad news, only to discover that he was away on an overseas business trip. A sudden realisation dawned on me, as I considered the difficult choice which now lay before me. I was presently committed to hosting Week Three of a seven-week seminar, which I had been planning for several months. To postpone it for a week or so was not viable because the guest speakers, who were travelling from far and wide, had had the date of their talk and its topic in their diaries for months. It now seemed I had no choice but to cancel the seminar, which I may not be able to set up again for several months, if at all.

Taking my dilemma to prayer, I asked the Lord what I should do. The reply was both startling and shocking at the same time. Into my mind came the words from Scripture, *"Let the dead bury their own dead!"* Surely this could not be right. It would go against the Fourth Commandment to 'Honour thy father and thy mother.' So, what did the Lord Jesus mean by,

"Let the dead bury their own dead" (Luke 9:60).

Did the answer lie in the continuation of Jesus' reply *"...but you go and proclaim the kingdom of God."* In my context, I could see this as meaning to continue with the seminar. But would it be dishonouring my father to make this a priority? I was deeply puzzled.

At this point, memory served to bring an answer. A homily I once heard based on this Scripture, emphasised the significance of the two words, "But first" in each of the replies from the hearers of Jesus to "Follow Me." It does not mean that we should ignore our sacred responsibilities towards our parents but it is just another way of saying, 'Put your spiritual responsibilities to God before all other duties.'

The second memory was of an occasion during mine and Tom's courtship when, declaring his love for me, he astonished me by saying that I was number two in his life! *What!* I thought, then he took up his statement with an explanation. "You are number two in my life because God must be first!" I had never experienced such mature faith as that and was greatly challenged by it at the time. Now the same challenge was set before me. Who was first, my precious father or God? This was to prove the hardest choice!

Difficult as the decision was, I decided God must come

first so I contacted the Funeral Director in Manchester the next day to explain why I could not travel to Manchester until the day after the seminar.

If I had any lingering doubts about this decision, they were immediately put to rest when he assured me there was no reason to cancel the seminar because, since it had been a sudden death, there had to be a post-mortem, which would take several days, allowing me to go ahead with the seminar after all! Other arrangements could be carried out by telephone and taken up when David returned from his trip. Isn't God good and faithful? Had He not already proved to me that if we 'Seek first the kingdom of God and His righteousness, then all these (other) things will be given as well.'

By God's grace, the seminar went ahead and the next day we travelled to Manchester and stayed until after the funeral, clearing the flat for the next occupancy and finalising the funeral arrangements.

During that time, something quite remarkable occurred. I think I had gone to the newsagent for funeral cards to notify family and friends of the funeral arrangements, when I noticed in the greetings cards section one for birthday cards for 'Father.' Looking across, I was suddenly filled with a deep sadness at the thought of never again being able to send a card to Dad for his birthday. Why I had not hurried past the stand, I will never know, but I felt drawn to it like a magnet. To my surprise, there was also a single Father's Day card, which was odd because it was well out of season. This was January and Father's Day is in June.

I have always liked meaningful words on cards, so was

slightly intrigued to read this lone Father's Day card. The words on the card just blew me over and I had to buy it.

A few days later, we were informed by the Funeral Director that Dad's body was now in the Chapel of Rest for viewing. I had only ever seen one deceased person before, and it had been a frightening experience, so I was more than a little apprehensive now. I was not even sure I wanted to see him lying in death. Better to remember him in life, I thought, and the wonderful times we had together. But, encouraged and supported by Tom, we went in to view him and to honour him.

I am so glad we did, for it put my mind and heart at rest. He looked beautiful! His face was serene and at peace. He reminded me of the then Pope, Pope John Paul II, even to the detail of a buttoned cape over the shroud!

In awe, I knelt beside the coffin and wept, in sadness, yes, but also in gratitude for the wonderful father God had given me. Then, rising once more, I moved to the coffin and placed into his hands the Father's Day card, with its beautiful, heartfelt words, which were to the effect that having such a wonderful father made it easy for me to accept God the Father as my Heavenly Father. What a role model he had been in life. Now, it seemed as if the words on the card were crafted by God the Father Himself as a fitting tribute.

With our final tribute paid, we slipped quietly out of the Chapel of Rest, leaving Dad to continue his eternal journey and life with God and all his loved ones. On the headstone marking his grave, I chose the words "To know him was to love him."

SAINT JOSEPH'S GIFT
Nazareth 19 March 1985

How appropriate that this memory should come to mind on this, the actual feast day of St Joseph, in the special Year of St Joseph 2021, dedicated to him. The particular memory evoked is an occasion when Tom and I were on pilgrimage in the Holy Land with The Catholic Bible School in March 1985.

We were in Nazareth at the time and had the good fortune to celebrate Mass that day in The Church of the Annunciation. During the homily, the celebrant suggested that, just as we may consider the Blessed Mother as our spiritual Mother, so, too, we might look upon St Joseph as our spiritual Foster Father. This thought struck me forcefully because just a few weeks earlier I had suffered the loss of my own dearly loved Father.

As Mass progressed and time came to receive the Eucharist, the priest suggested we stay in our positions, forming a semi-circle around the sanctuary, and he would come to each one, placing a Host into our outstretched hands.

Just at that moment I had a vision, not of the priest distributing the Host, but in his place, St Joseph was standing before us, carrying the young Jesus in his arms. As he approached us individually, he placed the infant into each person's outstretched arms to experience for a few seconds what it really feels like to receive an embrace from Jesus. It was an awesome experience. St Joseph was sharing his dear Child with us! What is more, following the priest's homily, it seemed as if St Joseph were also offering to us (and to me especially in my loss) the gift of his Fatherhood!

Recalling this event many years later, I can now appreciate more readily St Joseph's fatherly influence in my life.

At the age of eleven, I passed the 'Scholarship' or 11+ examination and was awarded a place at St Joseph's Convent School in Manchester. When I went into school that day, waving the letter to show to my teacher, I saw disappointment on her face instead of the beaming smile she had shown to other girls as they brought in their confirmatory letters.

After settling the class, she left us for a moment, to consult with the Headmistress about my result. When she returned, she explained that the Head was going to challenge the result, reasoning that on my class performance I should have been offered a place at my school of choice, Notre Dame Grammar School for Girls.

The dispute continued for some weeks, eventually calling my parents into the equation. An agreement had been reached whereby I could be offered a place at Notre Dame under certain conditions. My education would be paid for by Manchester Education Department, but my parents would be charged for all educational materials throughout my education.

When this was explained to me, I was reluctant to put any additional burden on my parents, who were already suffering considerable financial hardship. So, I happily insisted upon their accepting a free place at St Joseph's. This is how I became "A St Joseph's Girl" by default! Or was it by 'divine design'?

Pauline, the St. Joseph's Girl

My time at St Joseph's proved a happy association and I was soon eager to take on the mantle of being "A St Joseph's Girl." We were encouraged to take considerable pride in our school, not so much in a personal way, but collectively, as representatives of it, although inevitably there was a good deal of personal pride as well.

Initially, the Terms of Admission called for the signing of a four-year contract, at the end of which we took the 'Central School Certificate', which was the leaving qualification at that time. Just as my contract was nearing its end the school status was changed, from a Central School to a Technical High School, and with this change of status we had the opportunity to sign on for a further three years to take 'O' and possibly 'A' Levels.

My parents agreed to sign on for an additional year, which I was grateful for because my education had been heavily jeopardised during the previous two years because of my many absences due to my mother's ill-health. Nevertheless, I managed to pass the Central School Certificate in 10 subjects, five with Distinction, four with Credit and one Pass, which my teachers considered a "very creditable success" given my circumstances.

I stayed on for a further year and much to the disappointment of my teachers, I decided not to sign on for 'A' levels. I thought the best option was to earn money to support the family because I could not realistically contemplate leaving home for three years to go to university, which had been the expectations of my Headmistress and teachers. In fact, when I announced my intention to leave at the end of the year, I had to run the gauntlet every time I went into my English class as my teacher, grasping me by the hand said to me, "Miserable, miserable girl," (for my decision to leave school).

At this point, St Joseph's influence breaks in once again. Unknown to me, my Headmistress had been in touch or had been contacted by the Manager of a French company in the centre of Manchester who was looking for a "St Joseph's Girl" to fill a vacancy. He said that he could rely on her being, "loyal, efficient, hardworking and diligent." Sister Margaret was quick to recommend me, because, in addition to my academic subjects, including French, I was proficient at shorthand and typing.

Meanwhile, I did leave school and was enjoying what would be my last summer holidays, when a letter arrived from Manchester Education Department requesting me to attend for an interview. The school had written expressing their disappointment at my leaving, thus foregoing the opportunity of higher education. The aim of this approach was to have one last attempt to try to persuade me to return to school in the new term. The outcome of the interview resulted in their agreeing with my school's assessment, since they also saw in me "university material." I was greatly surprised and very flattered by this turn of events but decided it would be prudent to stay with my decision to leave school and to support my family.

Between St Joseph and my Headmistress, Sister Margaret, my future was mapped out. At this point, Sister Margaret had one last card up her sleeve. She invited me to come to see her, offering me, potentially, the job at the French company. Knowing I had a love for the French language, she cunningly knew this would be a good bait to interest me. She also acknowledged that since she could not persuade me to stay on at school, she wanted to send me off to a good start in the world of work. If that is not a work of grace, I do not know what is!

After attending an interview with the General Manager, Monsieur Galzy, I joined CFAO – Compagnie Francaise de l'Afrique Occidentale and was placed in an office with three French speakers, which developed my French language skills. During coffee breaks, I became acquainted with other members of staff, and after a while made a particular friend of Anne, who eventually became my sister-in-law!

Time went by and Anne eventually invited me to meet her brother who was presently home from Germany on leave from the RAF. It was to be a blind date, but I could not have chosen better with both eyes open! He was a tall, young man of nineteen, extremely handsome, pious and a devout Catholic. The attraction

Tom in RAF, 1958

was immediate and mutual. We were perfect for each other and our friendship, conducted mainly through letters, soon blossomed into courtship, from courtship to engagement, and eventually to marriage.

Without my being a "St Joseph's Girl" we might never have met. I may have taken up another place of employment and my future would have taken a completely different trajectory.

I worked at CFAO for over six years, until the birth of our first baby, Stephen. Another Catholic girl, Cecilia, was to replace me and I trained her for my job. By the time I was leaving, we had become firm friends and stayed in touch after I left. Eventually, she and her husband-to-be, Tony, became godparents to our third child, Peter, cementing our friendship even further.

On reflection, the influence of St. Joseph has permeated so many aspects of my life.

Nowadays, I am much more aware of St Joseph, and in gratitude pray for one last favour from the saint we pray to for a happy and holy death, that he will be there at the hour of my death.

NEW DAWN CONFERENCE
WALSINGHAM
1985

My routine dental check-up was coming to an end, with the encouraging remark from the dentist, "Everything looks fine, I'll see you in six months' time," when I suddenly remembered the small lump I had noticed in my lower jaw. Pointing this out, the dentist's attention was quickly riveted to the offending spot I had indicated. Within seconds I was being ushered into a scanning room, where a scan was duly taken. I would be contacted by telephone of the results. Accordingly, within two days, the results were back, and I needed to go into hospital for further investigations and possible treatment.

Before the operation, the surgeon explained the risks of removing the lump, which was close to a major nerve in the jaw, and which if accidentally damaged could cause my mouth to drop to one side and/or cause a paralysis on that side of the face. It was all very scary, but I had been prayed with the night before and felt quietly reassured and calm that I was in God's hands, and all would be well.

Recovering from the anaesthetic the news was mixed. The lump turned out to be a harmless cyst, but unfortunately and worryingly, the surgeons had noticed several growths in my throat. Since this was not their area of expertise, I would be referred to another hospital for further investigations by ENT specialists and seen within two weeks.

That same year, 1985, I had booked a place at the New Dawn Conference in Walsingham and had been eagerly looking forward to attending it. Fortunately, it fell within the two-week delay of my investigation, so I was able to attend.

The Conference was the largest I had so far attended, catering for approximately two thousand people, accommodated in a large marquee. The atmosphere was buzzing with excitement and anticipation as delegates chatted and introduced themselves. Some people knew the keynote speaker from other Conferences, a priest from the Dominican Republic, who was reputed to have the Charismatic Gift of 'Words of Knowledge.' This enabled him to specify prophetically the movements of God within the people, sometimes resulting in a healing, sometimes the person would be given a new direction in their spiritual life.

I had never seen this Gift in operation before and was marvelling as healings and prophetic 'Words of Knowledge' were pronounced.

Surprisingly, one such 'Word' seemed to be addressed to me. The priest spoke of there being a woman at the conference who had recently been told she had growths in her throat, but they were even now being healed by Jesus! I could not believe that I should be singled out from a crowd of such great size, yet the details were so specific. Not wishing to presume that the healing was for me, I automatically checked in at the hospital for my investigations/treatment a week later.

Surprisingly, the day after my operation, the surgeon came to discharge me as they could find no sign of any growths! "Then why is my throat bleeding?" I enquired. He explained that the bleeding was the result of their having scraped and scraped to find any signs of the growths which had so obviously been noted by two dental surgeons during the dental operation! I went home that day grateful to such a gracious God!

PROPHECY AT THE PRIMROSE TEAS
July 1986

It was the turn of Yateley Union of Catholic Mothers to provide tea and cakes for an elderly group of local ladies known as 'The Primrose Teas,' and it was my first experience of assisting at this event.

Because of my inexperience, but advantageous height, I was delegated to stand alongside the tall urn, and to fill it with water as and when the water level dropped from its regular filling of tea pots.

The afternoon went smoothly enough, and it was a joy to see the pleasure such little effort on our part gave to the ladies, who showed their obvious appreciation.

After everything had been cleared away and everyone began to make their way homeward, I was taken by surprise to hear an inner voice say, *"Today you have served tea, but a day will come when you shall also stand and serve the people water."*

What could this message mean? I had no idea but committed it to memory.

Six months after this event, I was checking my diary and noted that I was double booked on a particular date. By this time, I had become a councillor on the Parish Council, representing Christian Unity. This was clashing with a Liturgy Committee meeting on the same evening. When I mentioned the clash to my husband, Tom, he immediately offered to attend the Liturgy meeting on my behalf.

At home that evening, I was keen to catch up on the outcome of the Liturgy meeting. They had been discussing the upcoming season of Lent and Father John had suggested that each member of the group create a liturgy using various biblical images representing the Holy Spirit. In my absence, I had been allocated the symbol of the Holy Spirit represented by water.

After considering several biblical passages, from both the Old and New Testaments, I finally settled for the well-known passage referred to as 'The Woman at the Well' mentioned in St John's Gospel, Chapter 4.

Friend Jenny and I soon set to work on planning the liturgy, each contributing our different gifts. Jenny, with her artistic temperament and strong visual gifts, came up with the idea of re-creating Jacob's well, featured in the story, as a visual aid and backdrop to the narrative, whilst I set to work on the commentaries and prayers. Soon, the well, which we made from strong cardboard covered with stone-effect wallpaper, started to take shape, looking quite realistic.

The outline of the liturgy soon started to take shape. One reader would read the whole passage, putting the story into context. A second reader, following the process of the conversion of the Samaritan woman, as she spoke to Jesus, would break the passage into the discourse between Jesus and the woman, followed by a commentary and prayerful reflection, following closely the conversion process as the narrative progressed.

At some stage, Father John came to see how I was getting on with my liturgy and to see if I needed any help. I shared with him the format and outline of the liturgy so far, which he seemed very pleased with, to which I jokingly concluded, "Thank you Father, but you ain't seen nothin' yet," as I ushered him into the adjoining room where Jacob's well was under construction. He was both delighted and astonished at our ingenuity and we returned to the lounge where our conversation had begun, and he enthusiastically entered into discussion about our preparations.

At one stage, Father John asked if our version of Jacob's well was just a mock-up, or was it a 'working well,' by which he meant would it have water in it. An idea was percolating in his mind, obviously. At that stage, we had not thought of such a possibility, but soon I warmed to his idea of inviting the people in the congregation to drink the 'living water' Jesus had to offer.

At this idea, I invited Father John to represent Jesus at the well and at the appropriate part in the liturgy to offer the chance for the congregation to respond, by drinking the water, which he would offer. At this point, Father John asked if I had a part to play in the liturgy. When I responded negatively, he was firm in his conviction that I should have a part in it, and, thinking logistically for a second or two, asked if I would pass to him individual cups for him to fill from the well, as he offered the 'living water' to each person.

It did not strike me immediately, but as the days went by and we considered how to turn our mock-up of Jacobs well, into a working well and Father John's suggestion for me to hand him individual cups for filling, the words given at the Primrose Teas came to the forefront of my mind: *"Today you have served tea, but a day shall come when you shall also stand and serve the people water."*

With this realisation, the necessity of the model appearing to be a 'working well' became of great significance and urgency.

It was at this point that Tom came up with the idea of using the plastic beer barrel he had once used in an attempt to make a home-made brew! We laughed at his suggestion initially, but since no better suggestion had so far surfaced, we requisitioned the barrel, once thoroughly sterilised, for this more noble purpose! It fitted perfectly into the well awaiting its insertion, and filling, just before the liturgy was due to begin.

All that was left to arrange was for an appropriate song for the musicians and singers to perform as the people made their way forward to drink the 'living water.' I knew an appropriate song, aptly named *Come to the Water,* which I had recently heard sung by the music group in a neighbouring parish. It had a very repetitive chorus, which could be quickly learned as people walked towards the well. It so happened that the group was free to assist in our liturgy, so we were all set to go.

The evening of the liturgy eventually arrived; we were well rehearsed, and prayers had been offered for the Holy

Spirit to use our efforts to touch the hearts of the people.

Needless to say, the evening exceeded all our wildest expectations. We thought there might have been some hesitancy on the part of the congregation to be actively involved in the liturgy, especially in walking forward to drink from the well! We need not have worried on that score; everyone went forward, picking up and joining in the singing of the chorus of *Come to the Water* as the music group sang the verses.

When the evening finally drew to a close with a concluding homily by Father John, the people did not appear to be in any hurry to leave and chatted for some time in the porch and patio area outside the church. In the meantime, because I was busy thanking the singers, musicians, and readers, I failed to notice that a line of children had started to present themselves for a drink from the well. When asked why they kept going back for yet another drink, they said it was because it "tasted sweet." None of the adults had this experience.

"Taste and see that the Lord is good." (Psalm 34:8)

FAYE:
FLIGHT FROM NEW ZEALAND TO
SYDNEY
April 1986

Moving down the aisle of the aircraft cabin I spotted my row, noticing a man already sitting in the window seat. My seat was beside him, in the middle, which would make it easy for the third passenger to get seated when they arrived.

I noticed immediately that the man was clearly upset, as he swept tears from his eyes, and I wondered what I should do next. Before I could do or say anything, he blurted out his anguish. He was from New Zealand but had been travelling back and forth to Sydney for work, returning home for the weekend every six weeks. He had just done this, for what was to have been a celebration of twenty-five years of marriage. Instead, he was utterly shattered to discover his wife had been unfaithful and wanted a divorce. The contrast between his situation and my own could not have been starker, for I would soon be travelling home to England to celebrate my own Silver Wedding with the renewal of our marriage vows.

Before he could say more, the passenger for the third seat approached, noticeably flustered as she looked for her row. Eventually, she was seated, and I introduced myself to her, then turned to the man once more to allow him to talk further if he so wished. He continued for a while in subdued whispers, perhaps, I thought, not wishing to share confidences with the other passenger.

Pre-take off instructions then boomed across the tannoy, diverting our attention momentarily. Once airborne however, I pushed back my seat so that I could readily look from side to side to listen to both travelling companions. Then Faye, as the lady was called, began to speak. She, too, was heartbroken because her 'partner', a term which was only just becoming fashionable, had just broken off their long-term relationship. How unlikely a situation is that, to have a passenger either side of me, each trying to process the same feelings of shock and rejection!

Initially, John and Faye compared their similar circumstances and as I listened, I noticed Faye's rings; almost every finger sported a very large and expensive-looking ring. My observation also took in the fact that she had apparently recently lost a considerable amount of weight, since the rings slipped up and down her fingers as she gesticulated to emphasise a particular point. Meanwhile, John was beginning to look somewhat bored. Was he perhaps feeling that my initial full attention to his story was now becoming overtly trained on Faye's circumstances? It was difficult to say because people can interpret the same set of circumstances so differently depending upon their previous experience, family background, religious and cultural differences, and general world view.

Whatever the reason, after only a short while, John indicated that he did not wish to discuss his problem with Faye and turned towards the window and stayed that way in a fixed gaze. Meanwhile, Faye took herself off to the toilets, emerging only moments later in an agitated state of panic and concern. One of her rings had slipped from her finger and had fallen down the toilet!

Once we were in level flight and the aircraft was on auto-pilot, my husband, Tom, came from the cockpit to check which seat I had been allocated. He was the Flight Engineer on the flight that day and we were travelling back from New Zealand after a short visit to see some long-standing friends from England. We were presently coming to the end of a three-month posting in Sydney with British Airways.

When Tom came along, I quickly alerted him to Faye's predicament and he promised he would radio through to Sydney to see what, if anything, could be arranged to retrieve the ring on arrival in Sydney. This calmed Faye somewhat. Meanwhile, she continued to fill in the details of her broken relationship.

Having listened carefully to her story, I felt I had little to offer by way of advice. How could I say, for example, "I know just how you're feeling" because I could not. However, I tentatively offered to tell her how I, myself, cope in difficult circumstances, starting with my belief and trust in God, the power of prayer, and repentance. This led naturally to the story of my conversion and the experience of being 'Baptised in the Holy Spirit.' From experience, I know this can sometimes immediately close down the other person, but not this time. Faye seemed drawn into what I was saying and the examples I gave, especially when I described the present-day renewal of the gifts of the Holy Spirit which many Christians are experiencing. Her reaction was immediate and somewhat defensive as she boasted of possessing, "much higher gifts," which I understood to mean 'superior' as she explained the reason for her confidence. She was a member of the Theosophical Society, ignorance of which momentarily closed me down.

Nevertheless, I wanted to defend my position, when surprisingly I heard the inner voice of the Holy Spirit whispering, "Don't evangelise." I couldn't believe what I was hearing but the words were emphatic, so I metaphorically 'retreated' and took up listening mode once again.

It is only a short flight of two and a half hours from Wellington to Sydney and the rest of the flight passed fairly quickly, with Faye asking questions of me and my beliefs. Soon the seatbelt sign was on again to prepare for landing and when it came time to say goodbye to my two companions, Faye clutched at my arm, as if her very life depended upon it, surprising me with the words, "I must see you again! I have never heard anyone speak about God as you do!" With only minutes to spare, I quickly gave her my telephone number, pointing out that we had only two weeks left in Sydney before our return to England.

Within a few days, Faye telephoned to make arrangements for us to meet again. I must say I was surprised that she had taken up my offer to meet again and, on the day, thought to myself *Now I will have an opportunity to speak in depth of my beliefs!* Once more, the Holy Spirit spoke, again with a warning, "Do not evangelise! Just listen, be with her where she is at." So, obediently, I listened attentively and compassionately for the remainder of the day, but just before Faye was about to leave, she again clutched at my arm, as she had done in the aircraft, this time requesting me to pray for her! Was this the Holy Spirit's timing?

I have not spoken so far about Faye's ethnicity. She was an Indian lady, so when she asked me to pray for her, I was apprehensive about her spiritual background, especially as I had never heard of the Theosophical Society. I was happy to pray with her, but I wanted to clarify that I would be praying to the Christian God, God the Father, God the Son, Jesus, and God, the Holy Spirit. At this point, she divulged the fact that she had been baptised and brought up in the Anglican faith in India but had become disillusioned with Christians. Ouch! With this revelation, I felt I could pray freely with her, knowing she understood my own Catholic background and was comfortable with my praying for her. After the prayer time, she left in a much happier frame of mind, it seemed.

Conscious that our time in Sydney was coming to a close, I checked my 'still to do list' and recalled a request from friends back home to look up someone they had met in Sydney at a 'Mega' church as it was called. I would have to do this as soon as possible, so I made plans to meet them there at the weekend. It was an awe-inspiring sight, with thousands of people crowding into a vast auditorium. As arranged, I met up with George and Joyce who knew our friends back home. They were a friendly couple and at the end of the service offered to drive me home in their car. It was during the car journey that I spoke about Faye, her connections with the Theosophical Society, and my ignorance of such. I explained my concern that there would not be sufficient time to follow up on Faye since Tom and I would shortly be returning to England. No sooner had I said this when George, said, "I'm your man, I have studied Theosophy. I would love to meet up with Faye and see where it takes us," adding with a wry smile, "You were the Evangelist; I'm the Teacher." (Referring to Ephesians Chapter 4, verses 11-12)

Before leaving Sydney, Tom and I accepted an invitation to Faye's home and explained about George's offer to meet up with her. The fact that George was knowledgeable about Theosophy played a significant part in her warming to the idea. She was grateful and completely open to meeting him.

As we spoke about the possibility of her meeting up with George, Faye was just about to add something when a sudden change came over her. One moment her eyes were looking straight at us; in the next they were no longer focusing anywhere in the room, as her eyes rolled upwards into their sockets and she fell into a trance-like state. Even her features looked different as they twisted and formed into various ugly contours, as if her face were made of plasticine. Then, there was a sudden onset of coldness in the room as this manifestation took place.

I knew I was not imagining it, for I caught sight of the alarm on Tom's face. He, too, was apparently registering it all just as I was. It felt sinister and alarming, altogether not a good place to be, but we were transfixed in the shock of it all.

I do not know if Tom was praying at that time but I certainly was and wondered how we could extricate ourselves from this horrific experience.

A few minutes went by (or was it merely seconds?) and then Faye's face started to return to normal, to our great relief. No words of explanation came from Faye, and we did not even know what to ask. We just sensed this was not a good place to be and made our excuse to leave as soon as possible, but not before Faye once more confirmed that she definitely wanted to meet George.

At this point, I began to realise why Faye, at our first meeting on the aircraft, had been so desperate to meet up with me again, and why she had later welcomed Christian prayer.

When we caught up with George later, we explained how our meeting with Faye had developed and he seemed not to be too surprised by it all. He still felt he would like to take Faye under his wing, so we kept in touch about her progress with an occasional correspondence once we were home.

To our great delight, news reached us that Faye eventually rejected the practices of Theosophy, which we later learned was a combination of Indian mysticism and Spiritualism, returning once more to her former Christian faith.

It never fails to astonish me how delicately the Lord weaves our lives into the lives of others. Who could have imagined that a short flight would so influence someone's life? The timing was perfect. If I had ticked off meeting up with George on my 'to do' list earlier in the posting, none of the pieces of this jigsaw would have been in place. Even the lost ring played its part in the drama, drawing Tom into this holy activity.

As for the ring? It was never retrieved and became for me a symbol of the old life Faye would leave behind when she re-converted to Christianity, reminiscent of the Samaritan woman who went to Jacob's well for water, met Jesus and in her haste to tell her neighbours left her bucket behind! (John, Chapter 4).

Some commentators read into the detail of the Samaritan woman leaving her bucket behind as representing the Samaritan woman leaving her old way of life behind, which I rather like. Just as for her a new life had begun, likewise for Faye.

CONVERSION AT 35,000 FEET
1986

Are you the type of person who, faced with a long flight, chooses not to get into conversation with the person sitting next to you, for fear of either boring them or being bored by them? Or do you like to engage with people and make the most of the shared journey? On different occasions, I can be either of these.

This was uppermost in my mind when faced with a very long flight. Finding myself seated next to a lady, I decided to do the courteous thing, introduce myself, then allow her to indicate if she wanted to engage in conversation. Since the flight would be a long one, from Sydney to London, once we were airborne, I quickly introduced myself, explaining the reason for taking this flight. Tom (who was in the cockpit operating the flight) and I were returning home to England after a three-month posting with BA in Sydney and were now looking forward to celebrating our 25th wedding anniversary the next month. My companion was only travelling as far as Zurich.

Conversation between us came easily and soon she was disclosing her reason for travelling to Zurich. She had been suffering from chronic back pain and had heard of a special clinic there where they had significant success in treating spinal problems and had booked in there for treatment.

As a former fellow back sufferer, I commiserated with her, mentioning that I, too, had suffered for many years. Immediately picking up on my use of the past tense, this sparked the question, "So what happened?" "I was healed by God" - not at all what she had been expecting to hear. Naturally, she wanted to hear more.

Before embarking on my case history, I pointed out that I had no intention of projecting my situation onto her by implying that our conditions were the same. With that proviso, I continued with the story of how my healing had occurred, how for many years I had been told my problem was not physical but psychosomatic (which basically means the body and soul are not in harmony). I dismissed this diagnosis and for a further seven or eight years suffered persistent, intense pain, but it was only when I had a deep conversion experience and was shown an image of the state of my soul through holding onto resentment, that I repented, lamenting my pitiful state, and was eventually healed.

She was intrigued to know more about the vision, so I shared the story of how I was shown a festering wound (a symbolic image of the state of my soul) through not forgiving certain individuals who had hurt me. I had judged them and held onto what I considered justifiable anger but once I repented of this, the vision changed, showing a deep wound, now cleansed, through my repentance. The third image showed the edges of the wound coming together as if by an invisible hand, closing the wound as it moved along. At a certain point, the vision ended, and I knew that the healing process had begun. Sure enough, within a very short time, two weeks or so, my back problems were gone.

The lady listened intently and thoughtfully for a long time, surprising me with her next comment. "We Catholics have the answer, don't we, in the Sacrament of Reconciliation?" Up to this point, she had not disclosed any religious affiliation, so I had no idea she, too, was a Catholic. She then went on to say that she was a lapsed Catholic and my story had moved her deeply.

The remainder of the flight passed pleasantly enough, with shared stories, but before she left the plane at Zurich, she promised that, regardless of whether she was healed there by medical intervention or not, on her return to Sydney she would go to Confession as soon as possible and renew her relationship with God and the Church.

The message I learned from that encounter is that we never know how a friendly introduction can spark a life-changing event in another person's life. This lady was looking for healing, and what she found was the doorway to wholeness of body and soul.

I shall never know the outcome of that chance meeting and I do not need to know. What I do know is that her life took a new direction at the prompting of the Holy Spirit, and the outcome is His responsibility, not mine.

A CALL TO PERSEVERE
Late 1986

For the first time since the Prayer Group was formed in 1980, there had been a break in continuity, when Tom and I went to Sydney on a three-month posting with British Airways, earlier in the year. Nobody had wanted to assume the leadership role in my absence, despite offering the use of our home for meetings, so the group had gone into abeyance.

On my return, we quickly regrouped and celebrated the reunion, but things were not the same. The members who used to travel each week from Farnborough, some five miles away, had used the time to set up a prayer group in their own parish. Whilst I welcomed their initiative, their absence had quite an unsettling effect on the already small mother group in Yateley, which was to be expected.

We had started out with only three founding members, so we were familiar with the dynamics being in a small group brings, but when a few others (from a different church) left, to become more active in their church, it certainly felt as if we were sitting around the dying embers of a once glowing fire.

One member, Ros, especially needed the continued fellowship and support of a group, so I took the situation to prayer to discern whether the dwindling numbers was the sign needed to disband the group, or whether we should continue. After all, I reasoned, we had always considered ourselves to be the Lord's group.

As I write this recollection, I am reminded of the famous reply attributed to Saint Bernadette of Lourdes, when asked whether she missed all the attention she received at the time of the apparitions of Our Lady, in comparison to the obscure life she was then living as a nun in the convent at Nevers. Her modest reply was, "I was merely a broom in the hands of the Lord for a time, and when He had finished, He placed it back in the corner." Such was our situation. As a group we had been used in many surprising ways in the past. The Lord had brought us into existence, used our little group for His purposes for a time, and maybe now, He had other plans.

On one occasion as I was pondering the situation while doing my housework, I suddenly experienced a strong twinge of pain in my back. Catching my breath as well as my attention as I momentarily slid down onto the settee for relief, it was then that the word 'Hebrews' came into my mind. Looking down on the floor beside me was my Bible, still resting there from the Prayer Group meeting the night before, so picking it up, I searched for the Book of Hebrews, not one I was very familiar with. Flicking through the Bible to locate 'Hebrews', it happened to open up in chapter ten, so I began to read from that point.

As if highlighted, which I tend to do with any Bible verse which catches my attention, the following verse seemed miraculously illuminated as my eyes fell on it:

"Let us not give up meeting together as some are in the habit of doing.
Instead, let us encourage one another all the more, since you see that the Day of the Lord is coming nearer"
(GNB Hebrews 10:25)

Here was the answer, so in response to the Lord's guidance and encouragement, the Prayer Group continued for a further three or four years. By then Ros had died and a new path lay before the remaining members and myself, as I enrolled to study for a Diploma in Pastoral Theology, which would allow me to teach adults, at Parish and Diocesan level, all aspects of the Faith.

A new chapter in my life was about to unfold. Just as the 1980s had been the decade of the Prayer Group, so the 1990s would prove to be one of much study. Firstly, to teach Adult Religious Education and later to qualify and work as a professional counsellor for the remaining ten years of my working life.

RUSSIA

LET MY PEOPLE GO
14 February 1987

Something of a pattern had started to emerge whenever I became aware of a prompting from the Holy Spirit. An important 'revelation' would often occur on significant dates, perhaps so that I might readily recall them. Such was the case when the following episode began.

I had just plucked up courage to share with Tom that I felt the Lord was calling me to Russia. He listened respectfully, withdrawing into his own inner world, to process the implications and his possible involvement in the venture. Never, even for a moment, did he doubt my sincerity and integrity. Had he not witnessed first-hand how such promptings in the past had developed into incredible journeys led by the Holy Spirit?

I was still applying my makeup in the bathroom when Tom called up to me excitedly from downstairs,

"Hey Honey, do you know what day it is today?"

"St Valentine's Day," I replied.

"No," he retorted with a feigned note of disgust in his voice, "It's the Feast of St Cyril and St Methodius!"

"And who are they?" I thought, as Tom went on to give me a

potted history of two Greek brothers, one a priest, the other a bishop, who are credited with taking the Gospel to the Slavs in the tenth century. By means of what we in the West know today as the Cyrillic Alphabet, this allowed the Slavic people to hear and read the Gospel in their own language. Cyril translated the Bible into Old Church Slavonic and invented the Glagolitic Alphabet based on Greek characters, which in its final Cyrillic form is still in use as the alphabet for modern Russia and a number of other Slavic languages. Tom had gleaned much of this information when he had opened up our daily spiritual readings, thus making obvious connections with my earlier revelation about going to Russia.

Meanwhile, I, too, was making my own connections, with an earlier vision of two doors opening, one with Chinese characters above it, the other with what I took to be Greek letters. Could it be that it was not the door to Greece opening up but, in fact, Russia? Events on the world stage certainly all pointed to this at the time.

Meanwhile, speaking of language, ever since Mikhail Gorbachev came into power in the Soviet Union in 1985, two words had entered into the vocabulary of the Western world: Perestroika meaning 'restructuring', referring to political and economic reforms, whilst Glasnost meant 'openness and transparency' which was an attempt to lessen the Cold War between the Soviet Union and the USA by agreeing to reduce their nuclear weapons' arsenals.

In this atmosphere of growing mutual openness and trust, it was hoped it would extend to religious tolerance.

Rumour had it that Gorbachev was sympathetic to this notion, having had a Christian grandmother. Perhaps the Communist regime was at last softening its attitude to religious practice after seventy years of prohibition. Instead of the need for Christians to meet surreptitiously in forests and graveyards, there was even talk of some churches opening for worship. By the time we went to Russia, there were obvious signs of restoration, with onion-domed churches newly gilded with gold.

In that changing world, when Perestroika and Glasnost seemed to be in the headlines most days, it was neither of these terms which captured my imagination, but another hardly ever mentioned Russian word, Refusenik the name given to anyone seeking to leave Russia, but usually applied to Jews wishing to return to Israel, and whose applications had been refused. The ensuing protest marches were quickly quashed, with persistent objectors labelled 'Refuseniks' and given heavy prison sentences. I had heard of their plight from Ruth Heflin whose ministry, in part, was set up to anticipate the return of the Jews to their homeland. This was all I knew about these unfortunate souls at that time; however, our little prayer group had been alerted to the cause of the Refuseniks through a prophetic vision given to one of our group members.

One evening, friend Jenny shared a surprising vision she had experienced during her prayer time, of a man with a long grey beard who appeared to be in prison. She had no idea who he was, but his face appeared to her several times, each time as if pleading for help. Having shared this with us, we decided to take the vision seriously and to pray for him, individually and collectively, despite not knowing who he was.

To return to this particular calling, Tom was sufficiently convinced about going to Russia to agree to setting the wheels in motion for this to happen. It wouldn't be easy to visit Russia as one would any other country. There were still heavy restrictions in place and a Russian visa had to be granted.

Just about this time, British Airways gained the route to Moscow and Tom, in his capacity as Flight Engineer, flew on one of the first flights to this destination. He saw this as a dry run for taking me on a trip with him, but strict regulations made this impossible. If I were to accompany him, we would have to take our place on a long list of applications, and fly by Aeroflot, the Russian airline. This explains the long delay since that first conversation in February and our eventual trip in October.

When Tom phoned the Russian Embassy to obtain a Russian visa, a quite remarkable thing occurred. At some stage in the conversation, the telephone was put on hold, whilst the person answering went away to check some details. To the amazement of both of us, when the courtesy music began to play while the line was kept open, the music issuing from the phone was the Christian hymn, *Thine Be The Glory*. We took this to be a second sign that we were on the right track in going to Russia, the first sign being the date I mentioned about Russia, on the feast of St Cyril and St Methodius.

We were not quite certain why we felt so drawn to travel to Russia, but we were further encouraged when, one night at a Prayer Group meeting, one of the members, prompted by the Holy Spirit, quoted the following Psalm:

"The Lord will watch over your coming and going"
(Psalm 121:8).

Following this prophecy, we felt reassured that everything had already been arranged, the places we would visit and the people we would meet. We need only be obedient and go!

With the visa came detailed information regarding how, where, when and with whom we would be escorted during our short visit. In the meantime, we had anticipated the need for warm clothing and appropriate footwear and had packed and prepared accordingly.

The journey itself had a rather embarrassing start for the proud Russian airline, when our flight was grounded for a few hours, while some purely routine servicing had to be carried out. Other than a rather shaky start, the flight to St Petersburg went smoothly. Incidentally, our destination was still named Leningrad at that time. Historically named St Petersburg, it was later renamed Leningrad (Lenin's city) shortly after his death in 1924.

Later, on 6th September 1991, the original name of St Petersburg was returned by a city-wide referendum.

An Unexpected Introduction to Russia
In those early days, when Russia was beginning to open its

doors to receive Western visitors, and in order to ensure absolute control of people, we were grouped in parties of seven, and assigned to a particular guide.

On arrival at Leningrad airport, we were introduced to a group of young American musicians, two young men and what I had understood to be their female vocalist, named Joanna Stingray. I wondered whether this was perhaps some reference to her incredible hairstyle, which stood up in spikes, each spike tinted a different colour! With her was her Russian boyfriend who did not speak a word of English, nor she any Russian. A young man representing a well-known instrument maker, completed their group. Finally, Tom and I were introduced to them and I am sure the young musicians groaned inwardly at being teamed up with a middle-aged English couple.

Soon, we were guided to a row of buses and when each was full, we were driven off to our hotel. Once there, papers were checked and re-checked for what seemed an age, which proved to be too much for one person from a group on the other side of the room.

We first became aware that something was wrong when screams of panic erupted from their group. Someone had collapsed suddenly and they were urgently calling out for medical attention. No one seemed to have first aid skills, so were panicking in case their cries for help could not be understood.

Taking in the seriousness of the situation, I did something I had never done before nor since. Although I had no medical training myself, I felt compelled to go and do the only thing I could for the man. I could pray for him.

When I approached, he appeared to be unconscious, was drained of colour, his lips had turned blue and no breathing was evident. Kneeling beside him on the floor, I prayed silently and waited for any response, either from the man or from God!

Within a few seconds of offering my prayers, there was what seemed like a sudden convulsion from the man as he took in a huge intake of air, gasped a few times, and eventually started to resume a normal breathing pattern. When eventually he opened his eyes, he stared up at me in amazement, with a questioning look in his eyes. Waves of thankfulness and relief washed over me in turn as we waited for professional help. At last, the paramedics arrived, checked him over but decided to take him to hospital for a further check. The next morning, I was both delighted and relieved to hear from his group members that he was fine. The story transpired that he had undertaken a long flight from Canada and had been drinking heavily during the flight. What an introduction to Russia!

That day, we breakfasted as a group and were eventually joined by Elena, our guide, who was very keen to get started. She escorted us to a 42-seater bus, reserved for just our group and we were taken on a city tour, showing off the Winter Palace and other examples of the city's beautiful architecture, designed to replicate buildings at the time of the French King Louis XIV.

With equal pride we were shown the uglier side of Russian history, the battleship Aurora moored in the Neva

River. Although it is now a museum piece, it was still an active commissioned ship of the Soviet Navy which, in 1917, fired the blank shot that served as a signal to storm the Winter Palace during the October Revolution. It turned out that we were there just a few days

Battleship Aurora in St Petersburg (formerly Leningrad)

after this event was commemorated on 7th October.

After lunch, Tom with two members of our group, travelled by bus and metro to the Pushkin Monument, then had a brief tour around the Russian Museum. I did not accompany them on this occasion, preferring to save my energy for what promised to be an incredibly entertaining performance by a famous Cossack group of dancers.

The sightseeing group later returned to the hotel, meeting up with the rest of us for an early meal, before setting off to see the famous Cossacks.

We had seen The Russian Army Cossack Troupe on TV but even that had not prepared us for a live performance. The bright red of their tunics, contrasting starkly with the black pants, fur hats, and knee-length boots, plus the sheer vibrancy, and speed with which various movements were carried out, often with the flash of swords swung and swished as in genuine sword fighting, fairly took our breath away. Certainly, it was an evening to remember.

Jewish Connections

When the show was over, we began to search for our bus to return to the hotel, among the many that were parked outside. During all the confusion, an American lady invited us to share her bus as there was plenty of room and we were all going to the same hotel. We jumped at the invitation, remembering how our bus had been full of French and German speakers. Once on board, Barbara our new contact, introduced us to her husband, Joe. They were from New York and were, in fact, Jewish! This unexpected and brief encounter proved to be a vital link in fulfilling the purpose for which we had been called.

Barbara and Joe's group had already visited Moscow, doing our trip in reverse order. Excitedly, they and other members of their group spoke about having visited the synagogue in Moscow to commemorate a special time in the history of their Faith. They spoke, in passing, that they were there to celebrate a special feast, and were greatly surprised when I filled in the momentary gap by announcing, "Yes, it's the Feast of Tabernacles, isn't it?"

At our obvious interest in their Jewish faith, they said we must visit the main synagogue in Moscow and provided us with details of its location.

It looked as if the prophecy given before we left England, that all was arranged, our 'coming in and our going out,' the places we would visit and the people we would meet, was beginning to be fulfilled.

The following day would be quite different. The bus was to be completely at our disposal since the remainder of our group would not be joining us that day. They were visiting Russia on their own mission - to promote 'Peace through Rock and Roll' and had been invited to the radio and TV studios for an interview, prior to giving live performances at some time in the future should the government sanction it. Gifts of keyboards from a particular well-known instrument maker, it was thought, would help to promote this.

As an aside, it was not until I was writing these memoirs some thirty-five years later that I learned what had become of Joanna Stingray. I am not sure about the other band members but Joanna herself had become instrumental in bringing underground Soviet Union rock bands to the attention of the Western world and music scene. She had produced an album in 1986 called *Red Wave: 4 Underground Bands from the Soviet Union*, which caught the attention of American musicians and artists, such as David Bowie and Andy Warhol. Perhaps even more significantly, when allegedly Mikhail Gorbachev learned that the album had been produced by a foreign (Australian) company, he instructed the Minister of Culture to permit the publication of music of young Soviet musicians inside the Soviet Union.

So that was her mission and quite an astonishing one at that, which I had not fully appreciated at the time but now recognise it as the ground-breaking achievement it was. It was somewhat different from our 'mission' to Russia, the purpose of which was, as yet, not fully apparent to us.

Now, back to Leningrad and 1987...

Mass in Leningrad

Tom and I had asked Elena the day before if it would be possible to attend Mass in a Catholic Church. She was very helpful in this regard and made enquiries for us and gave written directions to the driver to take us there.

The church Elena had indicated, was the only functioning Catholic Church in Leningrad, still thought to be something of a show church to demonstrate to Westerners the new openness to religious tolerance.

Having arrived a little early, no worshippers had yet arrived, but the priest must have heard us enter the church and popped his head around the door of the sacristy, where he had been preparing for Mass. Noting our presence, he gave a reassuring nod in acknowledgement, before returning to his preparations for Mass. Now was not the time for proper introductions; that would come later.

But we could not help noticing the cautious look on his face when he had first appeared; the same look which now crossed his face again as his eyes momentarily searched around the church, before returning once more to his preparations.

With those two disturbing expressions, we wondered, *"Who is he looking for? Who or what did he expect to see?"* They certainly introduced an ominous feel to the situation.

Within a short time, the people began to file in in silence, out of respect for the House of God and His Presence there, soon filling the small church to capacity, in pews on either side of a centre aisle.

What struck us forcefully was the devotion of the people

in that crowded church, mainly old people, who had held on tenaciously to their faith during the Communist era, despite persecution and many privations. Prayer books, which had been lovingly handwritten from memory, were dog-eared from frequent use.

Mass proceeded with its familiar and recognisable liturgy, the Readings for which we followed in our own missal (prayer book), making us ever grateful for the universality of our Catholic faith. (The same Readings are read throughout the world). Knowing this, we had brought our missals with us.

When Mass ended, we remained in our pew, allowing everyone to file out of church so we could take a closer look around.

It was then that we noticed two men standing at the back of the church observing the proceedings. We first noticed them when they presented themselves for Holy Communion and were shooed away with a gesture from the priest. These two men were not worshippers but KGB men, observing everything, we later learned.

Eventually, after satisfying themselves that we were, apparently, only tourists, the KGB men left and the priest re-appeared, staring at us enquiringly, again looking around to check that we were not observed. Then he beckoned to us to follow him into the sacristy. Once there, he held out his hands in a receiving gesture, at the same time attempting to question us, at first in Russian, then other languages, until we eventually found a common tongue in very limited French on both sides.

The only thing we had carried with us was a handful of medals and five Rosaries donated by one of the prayer group members. His gratitude for these items was obvious but we could see it was mixed with disappointment as he checked if we had brought any Bibles. Rosaries they could make for themselves, he explained, but a single page of Scripture was precious and could be lovingly translated and duplicated.

I had met this hunger for Scripture before when I travelled to China, on that occasion carrying (smuggling) a holdall containing thirty bibles.

It so happened that we had with us our own family bible - nothing elaborate in itself, just a simple copy, but precious to us in its own right, for it contained Tom's entries of significant dates, from our wedding up to and including the Baptismal, Confirmation and First Holy Communion dates of our three children. We had carried all our religious items with us, not wishing to run the risk of having them confiscated if found in our hotel room.

These dear people had been denied access to Scripture and religious objects for over seventy years, and their hunger was understandable. Their need for a bible was greater than ours, so we finally parted with both missal and bible. These the priest gratefully accepted, clasping them close to his chest to express his thanks, for he had no words with which to do this adequately.

Gaining 'Street-cred'

We returned to the hotel just in time for lunch, before another sightseeing tour of the city. By the evening, we were so exhausted from all the earlier activities we were rather relieved to hear that it was not possible to attend the theatre later, for some unspecified reason. So, we spent the evening dining with our group, after which, one of the musicians invited us to join them for a game of Ten Pin Bowling in the hotel, which he had already booked.

Although neither Tom nor I had ever played, we were prepared to give it a shot. The first thing I noticed, and commented upon, was the heaviness of the bowling ball. As a result, when I attempted to hurl mine down the alley, it barely trundled along. But my aim was sure and all the pins went down! "Beginner's luck," the cry went up, but as the game progressed and my turn came to bowl again the same luck prevailed. I had now certainly gained considerable street cred by scoring not just one, but two strikes!

It had been a very full day. Tomorrow would be our last day in Leningrad and we had a long overnight train journey to Moscow.

Before leaving Leningrad, we were taken for one last sighting of the Aurora moored at the quayside, which gave an open view of the Gulf of Finland, an escape route taken by many a fleeing Refusenik in the past, and in the future too, we prayed.

The Train Journey to Moscow

The nine-to-ten-hour journey from Leningrad to Moscow might have proved a little awkward, but for two seemingly insignificant occurrences. Awkward because up to this moment we had not shared much time at close quarters with our travel companions. They had not joined us on sight-seeing trips because they were in Russia with a different objective. The thought of being cooped up together in a train compartment for so many hours was a little daunting, but we need not have worried.

Travelling by coach to the station, our musical friends started singing some well-known pop songs of the day and I joined in, which surprised them, and they complimented my singing! With my successful double strike at Ten Pin Bowling the night before, a little more street cred and acceptance into their world was being notched up.

Mounting the train, we were guided to two cosy compartments, each with its own little stove situated beneath the window and two double bunks on either side. Initially, we all spilled into the first compartment and soon Joanna and her boyfriend had climbed onto one of the top bunks, dangling their legs over the edge, looking very much like a pair of roosters in a hen coop. Two of the boys from the group claimed the lower bunk, leaving the other one sharing the edge of one of our bunks on the opposite side. I had begun to notice this was the usual configuration that the group took whenever they had to split up. It was the case when bed spaces were decided upon later, leaving the remaining member of the group, whom I shall call Brad, sharing our compartment.

Conversation flowed naturally and comfortably between the musicians and soon we, too, felt included. Singing broke out from time to time, interspersed with the re-telling of anecdotes and reminiscences. Thus, we passed several hours until, like the dying embers in our little stove, individuals started to 'call it a day,' to retire. Before doing so, however, Brad became aware of the tune I was gently humming. "Is that *Amazing Grace* you are singing?" With my affirming nod of the head, he called for attention from the group. "Hey, we've sung just about everything else, why not let us end the evening with *Amazing Grace*?" Picking up their guitars one more time to accompany the singing, together we gave a heartfelt rendition of the familiar hymn. It was a perfect ending to the evening, so it seemed, but it proved to be not quite the end. All except Brad made their way to the other compartment, leaving Brad still sitting beside me. He had questions to ask.

Amazing Grace
Looking rather uncomfortable, he posed an awkward question, "What is it with you two? We've been puzzling over you ever since we met up. There's something special about you two."

Where could I start to answer such a question? Was it the singing of *Amazing Grace,* which had brought about this sudden reflective mood?

"If you can see anything special about us, it is the Holy Spirit living in us." Further questions followed this explanation and soon I was telling him my conversion story and subsequent experience of the Baptism in the Holy Spirit. Tom, meanwhile, had already indicated that he was tired, so I encouraged him to scramble up into the top bunk and leave me to answer the many questions, which were flooding Brad's mind.

My earlier explanation about my experiences of the Holy Spirit had intrigued him. In his childhood, he had grasped the notion of God the Father, and God the Son (Jesus) but God the Holy Spirit? You could even hear people still referring to God the Holy Spirit as God the Holy Ghost, frightening to his mind as a child and confusing even to adults.

It was necessary to recall the times in the Old Testament when we first hear of the Spirit of God, through to the time of Jesus when He promised to send the Spirit to all who believed. This occurred at the feast of Pentecost, when the Holy Spirit hovered above the heads of the Apostles in the form of flaming tongues of fire, after which they received special charisms, or gifts. I went on to mention some of the gifts outlined in 1 Corinthians, Chapters 12 and 14, and elsewhere throughout the New Testament.

My own conversion and first actual experience of the Holy Spirit never fails to touch people and it had this same effect on Brad, especially when I described how I had to forgive someone before I could receive the Holy Spirit. This account usually resonates with people, for who of us has no one they need to forgive?

One of the Gifts I received is the gift of visions and dreams through which the Holy Spirit began to speak to me.

Brad was captivated by what I shared about my conversion experience. He had never appreciated that God, through the Spirit, is speaking and guiding us every moment of our lives.

"How does this come about? How can you hear God? How do you know it is God speaking to you? Is the bible actually the Word of God?"

My response to each of these questions led to my sharing a particular episode in my life when these same questions had been asked by me and answered in remarkable, if not miraculous ways, some of which are recorded in these pages.

It was now Brad's time to speak.

He went on to tell of an experience in his own life, when he had miraculously survived a shoot-out in a bungled bank robbery, although he had not attributed his survival to God's intervention at the time. In fact, having already stopped the practice of his Catholic faith, he never expected any assistance from God. The surfacing of this long-suppressed memory brought with it a sense of gratitude and with that, happy associations with his former faith life.

Many questions went back and forth until, apologising for keeping me up so late, he thanked me, promising to look into his faith once more on his return to the States, this time with new eyes. Hopefully, Brad had begun to travel by another road that night, a road less travelled.

The train chugged on, stopping, it seemed, at every station, until we reached Moscow in time for breakfast.

Moscow
Despite the long overnight journey, we were keen to explore the city with its unique history and many historical monuments, so after checking in at our new hotel to freshen up, we joined Svetlana, our Moscow guide, in the lobby for a tour.

The tour took in famous landmarks, such as the Kremlin,

Red Square, and the tomb of Lenin. We were rather relieved that we were not expected to join the long queue to visit Lenin's tomb. Instead, Svetlana allowed us to walk around freely, arranging a meeting place an hour later, during which time we walked around the Kremlin walls, praying for the release of the Refuseniks and religious tolerance

Tom in Red Square Moscow 1987

in general. There we were, right at the heart of government and the seat of Soviet power, but we had a different agenda; we were there to pray for the restoration of civic and religious freedom.

Ballet in the Kremlin

When we met up with the coach after our preamble around Red Square we made a city tour, passing the theatre and home of the Bolshoi Ballet Company, which at that time was closed and boarded up. We looked at the building with dismay because according to our itinerary we were due to see a performance of the Bolshoi during our visit. Encouraging news came a little later, however, that alternative plans for a performance in the Palace of Congresses, right within the Kremlin walls, had been arranged.

Early that evening and accompanied by two of the

musicians, we set off for the State Kremlin Theatre Palace. Formerly known as the Kremlin Palace of Congresses, it is a large modern building inside the Moscow Kremlin.

A few facts might be appropriate here. Built in the 1960s as a place for Communist Party meetings, it was reputed to be one of the best and most prestigious concert halls in Moscow. For the last four decades, it has become the iconic landmark of Russia.

It is said that a visit to the Kremlin Palace is a remarkable event for anyone who visits and for us it was no exception. The main hall can hold six thousand people and its acoustics were considered to be the most advanced at that time. Over the years, this was the main place for the State public events and many Communist Party Congresses.

With some of these facts whirling round in our heads, imagine the excitement on entering such a place, not to mention the thought of enjoying a performance of *Swan Lake* by possibly the most famous ballet company in the world.

We were not disappointed. The strains of the orchestra, even as it played the overture, were magical. The curtain remained closed initially while the musicians played the overture, creating mounting anticipation as it was slowly raised.

I am no expert in acoustics; I only know that the music had me transfixed. As for the dancing - what can I say? I was completely enraptured, and to do justice to their performance would be to run out of superlatives, but if I had to choose just one, it would be exquisite!

Tom, who was very fond of classical music, once commented to me that to listen to the music of Tchaikovsky and other Russian composers is to give you a glimpse of the Russian soul.

We processed what we had just experienced as we made our way back to the hotel.

Talk about from one extreme to another, or even one world to another - we then managed to meet up with the rest of our group at the gym later that evening, where they were playing Ten Pin Bowling. We joined them in this pursuit and were all enjoying the game, when, without warning, the lady supervisor of the gym switched off all the lights. Our bowling companions were furious! It was customary etiquette where they came from either to allow the game to finish or give permission for the last players to switch off the lights.

Taking themselves off to drown their sorrows, the musicians made their way to one of the bars to round off the evening, but we took our leave, tired as we were, having had little rest after the long overnight journey.

Peace through Rock and Roll might be a possibility, but not likely, it seems, through Ten Pin Bowling!

Visit to a Synagogue
A surprise awaited us at breakfast the next morning at the sight of two of the musicians who we had previously only seen in casual attire now dressed in smart business suits. They had important business meetings with government officials, to negotiate the possibility of performances by

the group on future visits, and were urgently informing Lara, our new guide for that day, of their need of a car and chauffeur for the day.

When Lara realised that she would only have Tom and myself to escort that day, she became quite fractious and sulky, breaking into a mixture of English and Russian expletives, from what we could gather. Apart from the fact that we were her only takers for sightseeing, I cannot begin to guess why she was so upset.

We had hoped that Svetlana had passed on to Lara our request to include a visit to the Synagogue, but, anxious not to cross her nor raise her curiosity too much, we waited patiently while she attended to the boys' request.

As it turned out, Svetlana had forgotten our request so, angry at her colleague's ineptitude, and further frustrated by her own inability to find out the times of the synagogue services because there was no telephone connection, she finally announced that we could go there alone with the driver for the morning. Imagine, a whole 42-seater bus just for us!

We Meet a Refusenik
As we approached the synagogue, the driver indicated where he would wait for us and we made our way through the bustling crowd of worshippers arriving for the service. As we approached the steps, a man dressed in what could only be described as rags, tugged at my sleeve, holding out a long fingered, bony hand for alms. But it was his emaciated frame and the condition of his teeth, literally rotting in his

mouth, which attracted my attention.

Attending to the man's begging gesture, I placed some money into his hands and quickly caught up with Tom, who was gallantly forging a way for us both to enter the building. Closely following Tom, I failed to realise that women were expected to make their way to the balcony area above, from which they could observe the proceedings below.

Suddenly, I felt a strong tug on the collar of my jacket. It was the synagogue official, pointing to the mezzanine level above. Quickly following his directive, I made my way up the staircase, not knowing if Tom had seen this manoeuvre, but hoping he had. I need not have worried; Tom had seen it all and had taken in the implications when he noticed the all-women group on the balcony.

From our respective vantage points, we followed the proceedings with interest, though with little comprehension. What we were witnessing was the synagogue ritual associated with the Feast of Tabernacles, a harvest festival, when the Jewish people remember their time in the wilderness on the way to the Promised Land.

Because we were ignorant of its significance at the time, the experience encouraged a desire to know more about our 'Fathers in Faith' so when we got home, we started to introduce our fellow parishioners to some of the Jewish rituals, especially the most important one, The Passover Meal.

Just as we caught up with each other at the back of the synagogue on leaving, the synagogue official called us into a side room. Thinking we were about to be reprimanded for my earlier faux pas, we were pleasantly surprised when he thanked us for our visit, asking us to come again the next day, if possible, when, apart from the closing of the Feast of Tabernacles, many people would be gathering in solidarity and in silent protest at the plight of the many Refuseniks in the city, one of whom I had just encountered on our way in. So, that was a Refusenik! What a tragic plight.

A Final Visit

Having been told more about this underclass of Russian society, we naturally wanted to help in whatever way we could, so that evening we started to formulate a plan, but first, we needed to find a way to get to the synagogue. We did not see Joanna and the others that night, so had to wait until breakfast to tell them of our plans for our final day, indeed in order to bid them farewell, a safe journey home and the best of luck for all their future aspirations.

Lara had put aside her sulks of the previous day and we had a pleasant breakfast together. By then, she knew that the two musicians who we had seen in business suits the day before needed a taxi again that day to take them to their negotiations with the media world so, pleasantly this time, offered us the use of the bus to take us back to the synagogue!

We knew that this visit had a very different purpose and there was little time to waste. Squeezing our way through the crowd, we made straight for the little side room where we had seen the synagogue official the previous day. There he was, just as we had hoped, and we explained our concern for the plight of the Refuseniks and our wish to help in whatever way we could. The evening before, we had formulated a plan. When packing our bags for our return to England, we had dressed that morning with as many layers of clothing as we could manage under our equally bulky topcoats, which had proved entirely unnecessary for the trip as the weather had been unusually mild all week. In the presence of the synagogue official, we stripped off all our excess layers and donated these for the use of the Refuseniks – also leaving most of our remaining currency, which we no longer needed, since this was our last day.

Our gesture was greeted with both gratitude and disbelief.

Leaving the synagogue, we noticed the people outside had grown into a sizeable crowd, in a joyful pleasant mood, singing and dancing on the final day of their great feast until, at a signal, the crowd grew silent to make their peaceful protest on behalf of the Refuseniks. Once the silence was over, the people started to melt away and we, too, took our leave of these courageous people.

Let My People Go

One notorious Refusenik, we later learned from an article in a daily newspaper, was Yosef Begun. This was how we came to identify the person for whom the prayer group had been praying.

Yosef Begun became a Refusenik when he applied to emigrate to Israel in 1971, and his application was refused. He was repeatedly arrested for his political activities advocating for the free emigration of Soviet Jews to Israel, which ultimately resulted in his serving several prison sentences over a period of 17 years, including being exiled to Siberia.

In 1982, he received a seven-year sentence for 'anti-Soviet agitation and propaganda' (Wikipedia). His actual crime was writing descriptions of the situation of the Soviet Jews, which the authorities deemed to be anti-Soviet. His case resulted in wide protestations in the West by National Council For Soviet Jewry (NCSJ) and United States diplomats. In media coverage of his case, he was described as a 'Leader of the Jewish Emigration Movement.'[1]

In February 1987, Refusenik protests against Begun's continuing imprisonment took place in downtown Moscow and it was at these protests that some of the Refusenik protesters, including members of Begun's own family, were attacked and beaten by KGB agents in plain sight of onlookers and foreign journalists.

A short while after, on 16th February 1987, Begun was released from prison and was granted permission, with the other Refuseniks, to emigrate to Israel. However, Begun refused to leave without his whole family and it was not until January 1988 that he finally made it to Israel.

Like a modern-day Moses figure making his demand to the Pharaoh of his time, so Begun had shaken his fist at the modern captives of his people. Once more, the cry of "let my people go" finally prevailed, opening the way for the Jewish people to enter once more into their Promised Land.

Two years later, on pilgrimage, Tom and I had the thrill of

---

1 King, Wayne, and Irvin Molotsky. *"Rally for a Soviet Jew."* *The New York Times. January 31, 1987.*

seeing some of these former Refuseniks in Jerusalem itself.

And who would have thought that by 1991, the mighty Soviet Union would have been dismantled, without a single shot being fired? Had we witnessed history being repeated? In the pages of Scripture, we read how the walls of Jericho came tumbling down after the Israelites, following the command of God, simply marched around the walls seven times, praising God, after which the walls collapsed. With the collapse of the Soviet Union, the symbolic, if not the actual, walls of the Kremlin had likewise fallen.

Even today we are walking in, standing on, and surrounded by answers to prayers prayed in the past by others. For the unbeliever, no explanation is possible. For the believer, no explanation is necessary.

"More things are wrought by prayer than this world dreams of" - Alfred, Lord Tennyson

INDIA

CALL TO ASHLAND, VIRGINIA
April 1988
Park Place Pastoral Centre

It was April 1988 and Tom and I were especially looking forward to attending a weekend Bible Conference organised by the Catholic Bible School with Ruth Heflin, as keynote speaker.

The day before the Conference, Tom was called out on duty to replace another Flight Engineer who had become unwell. I was slightly apprehensive about driving to Portsmouth on my own, also not knowing anyone at the Conference. Nevertheless, I overcame my anxiety and drove to the venue.

On arrival, we were given a name badge to facilitate communication between the conference delegates. Despite my name, Pauline, being clearly displayed on the badge, during the course of the next few days, two different people called me 'Margaret' by mistake. Bemused by this, I brushed it aside. Finally, as the weekend was closing with Mass, this was to happen yet again, as the person distributing Holy Communion pronounced the words, "The Body of Christ,

Margaret" when I went up to receive the Eucharist.

Still pondering all this, I made my way to the dining room, where coffee was being served. Sitting down at the nearest available table, I found myself sitting next to another delegate, whose name happened to be – yes, you have guessed it, Margaret! She noticed the look of amusement which crossed my face as I explained what had been happening and how bewildering it all was since I was not known by any of these delegates. Even more astonishing is the fact that Margaret is actually my first name, though I am never called by it. I have always been known by my second name, Pauline, my mother's preferred name for me.

Without a moment's hesitation, Margaret said, "I believe the Lord is calling you, by your name." Since nobody but the Lord at the conference knew my first name, He had caught my attention by using it. That seemed a plausible explanation, but calling me for what purpose? To tell the truth, I had never liked the name since being unfavourably compared to a cousin of the same name. I thought maybe the Lord now wanted to deal with this resentment. Margaret continued, "Don't you know what your name means?" I pleaded ignorance. She explained that it means 'A Pearl.' "What is more," she chided, "you should treasure the fact that the Lord should be calling you by that name!"

Once the goosepimples had disappeared following this explanation, we then filed into the hall, where Sister Ruth began to minister. One of her Charismatic gifts was the Gift of Prophecy, when she would sometimes be given a message or an image from God for a particular person during prayer ministry.

In the queue, there were about ten or so people in front of me when, unexpectedly, Ruth looked up from praying with someone and beckoned me forward. She then whispered in my ear as I approached her, that the Lord had just dropped a picture into her mind of me in Ashland, Virginia. She could give no additional information other than that the Lord wanted me to go there, but by the time I went forward for prayer, she had further insight. The purpose was to release me into a particular ministry, for which the Lord was preparing me.

I was bewildered by all that was happening, but Ruth calmed my fears somewhat by inviting me to go to Ashland in July during the two weeks she would be there. I would be her guest.

The mere thought of driving myself to the conference had filled me with dread, so imagine the terror racing through my mind at the thought of making my way to Ashland, Virginia, alone. This would involve flying to Washington, then changing not only flights but changing airports as well! I had flown to many parts of the world with Tom and the family, but always there had been Tom to shepherd us all along. Panic clutched at my throat whenever I thought of the prospect, yet I knew I must answer the call.

In fear and trepidation, therefore, and in the light of all that had occurred at the conference, especially the specific prophetic vision given to Ruth, I went in obedience. This was certainly taking me well out of my comfort zone, but I would go, trusting in the Lord's providence. In Ashland, I would meet two people through whom God would point the way forward, in what was to prove an exciting and incredible adventure.

GLORY IN ASHLAND
July 1988
Summer Camp

Time finally came round for me to travel to Ashland. I had had no further word from Ruth in the meantime, but I had gone ahead and arranged my flight tickets and was ready to set out. The journey to Washington passed pleasantly enough despite there being no interesting fellow passenger prepared to share part of their life story, as so often happened to me when travelling. Some of these encounters are documented elsewhere.

Arriving at Washington, there were several hours to pass before my connecting flight to Ashland, giving me plenty of time to make any necessary enquiries. Eventually, I boarded the smallest aeroplane I had ever seen. It seated only about a dozen people and was so flimsy in comparison to the huge Jumbo Jets in which I was used to flying with Tom. It was fairly flung about the sky as we made our way to Ashland airport, often dropping suddenly a thousand feet or so! I was glad when we finally touched down. After such hair-raising experiences during the flight, I immediately started to dread the return journey!

Another problem then surfaced. After collecting my luggage from the carousel, I suddenly realised I did not know who, if anyone, would meet me at the airport. I had forwarded my itinerary to Ruth weeks ago but had not had a reply before setting out. How would I recognise the person sent to collect me? All I could do was to wait around for someone to approach me. Feeling like a piece of left luggage, I tried to make myself as comfortable as possible seated on a plastic airport chair, along the back wall of the Arrivals Hall. Thankfully, eventually, someone approached me, and after a fifteen-minute journey by car, I arrived at the camp.

News of my arrival was passed through to Ruth, who surprisingly did not come herself to meet me. She was the speaker that evening and was resting. I was taken to a part of the house where guests stayed, shown to my bedroom and from then on, I had to find my way around the site as just another delegate. I did not even have meals with Ruth and her family, as I might have expected, instead I ate in the large dining tent with others. This allowed me to mix with other people from different parts of America and around the world. As it so happened, the only person I met from England was an Indian lady, Maureen, from London.

The only time I saw Ruth was when she was the speaker for the afternoon or evening session. I found this a little odd but eventually realised the intention behind this. Faithful always to the prompting of the Holy Spirit, Ruth was allowing the Holy Spirit to reveal the purpose for which He had called me to Ashland through Ruth's vision in England.

I had arrived at the camp the day before the conference officially opened and there met another delegate, a pastor from Madras, India. He told me that in 1983, the Lord began to call him into his present work, which was to establish a home for destitute and poor (not necessarily orphaned) children. He had no idea how this would be accomplished, but he went on believing what the Lord had promised him and in time he was able to build a mission centre and slowly but surely, a handful of people were baptised each year and became Christians. Ten or so may not seem a large number but to change faith and become a Christian takes great courage, because sometimes that person is shunned, and quite often beaten up by their family if they convert to Christianity.

Significantly, 1983 was the very same year when I had been invited to celebrate St Peter's feast day at St Peter's Church in Yateley, and the Lord gave me a vision of a white cow and the word 'India.' I had no idea what it meant at the time, but the Lord had dropped it into my heart, and it would become clear in due course. It would take a further five years before our paths would cross, in Ashland.

Once the conference began, every day was filled with incredible teaching and praise. Pentecostals certainly knew how to praise the Lord! On more than one occasion, prophetic utterances spoke of the 'Shekinah Glory' (God's Divine Presence) descending upon us as they flowed in the charismatic gifts of prophecy, healing, and teaching. With such experiences, my days were gloriously filled.

One evening, I experienced a strange phenomenon in my

bedroom. I had switched off the light, throwing the room into pitch blackness. I was not used to such dense blackness, but we were right out in the country with no streetlights to shed their brightness, ideal for any astronomers who might be scanning the sky that night.

After lying there in this inky blackness, suddenly in the room there was what seemed like glowing dust particles, swirling as if being moved by a gentle breeze. I lay there, transfixed for some time, wondering if or when this cloud of bright particles would cease their movement or even disappear. But the moving cloud remained. Intrigued, I went to the only possible light source in the room, the tiny window behind my head. Swishing the curtains to one side, I expected to find the light source creating the growing bright cloud of glowing particles.

As might have been expected, given the location of the camp, I peered out, only to find the same inky blackness. The glow was in my room!

Strange though this experience was, and certainly well out of my frame of reference, I was not afraid. Instead, a sense of peace flooded my heart and I finally drifted peacefully off to sleep.

I awoke the next morning refreshed from a good night's sleep and headed off in the direction of the breakfast tent. As I walked along the path, another couple were walking in my direction. Anticipating a friendly exchange, instead the couple gasped, "You've got the glory on your face, your face is glowing!" Was this the 'Shekinah Glory' spoken of at the prayer meeting the previous night? Was that what

I had experienced in my bedroom? No other explanation came to mind. I had experienced the very presence of God, preparing me for a ministry.

During my stay in Virginia, it was again repeated in prophetic messages that I was being prepared for a new ministry, which I understood to be involvement with the Indian pastor's mission.

With these thoughts hurtling around in my mind, I finally had the opportunity to share with Ruth about my meeting with the pastor from Madras. It so happened that the day of my departure coincided with Ruth being guest speaker at a Men's Breakfast in Washington. So, instead of the bumpy flight from Ashland to Washington, I had a comfortable ride in Ruth's car, giving me time to catch up with her about my various experiences, and the making of new acquaintances. She confirmed I had experienced the Shekinah Glory cloud. I felt honoured and affirmed.

A PROPHETIC DREAM -
A CALL TO INDIA
Spring 1989

The story of the Call to Ashland seemed for a time to have been without purpose, and might have ended there, but for a disturbing dream. More than twelve months had gone by since meeting the pastor from Madras, and India was certainly not on my mind, when the dream occurred.

Not knowing the geographical position of Madras on a map, I could not have told you where it was located, but in the dream, I knew myself to be in south India and was being faced with a challenge. In front of me, was a very small, flimsy, fragile-looking, single-seater plane, which appeared to be my only means of travel. Suddenly, Tom appeared, in uniform, and my heart relaxed, thinking that he would now take care of the situation. But his words did not comfort me at all, as he said, simply, "I can't help you, Pauline. You have to do this yourself." With that he disappeared, and I was left, feeling terrified.

Still within the context of the dream, my thoughts darted here, there and everywhere, as the seriousness of my plight impacted upon me. Questions began to surface in my mind. After composing myself to a degree, I began to consider, *Supposing I were to pluck up sufficient courage to attempt to fly the plane, I could still get lost in thousands of square miles of Indian Ocean. How would I navigate?* At that moment, a voice answered in reply, "Just head out!" to which I replied, "Where will my refuelling stops be?" Again, the voice insisted, "Just head out!" There, the dream ended. Waking suddenly with a start, I was relieved to find it was only a dream. Or was it?

Lying in bed, my thoughts were racing ahead, visualising geographically the route from India to England, as I fancifully pondered the slim possibility of flying all the way back to England, if I could only keep sight of land! I really took the dream that seriously.

Staying with us at that time was a guest from Austria, so attempting to put these thoughts behind me and wanting to get a head-start on breakfast preparation, I went downstairs early but found Gabi already up and about.

Despite all attempts to push aside the dream, I was still fully emotionally charged by it, as I tumbled out its contents to her. Having shared with her about my call to Ashland when she stayed with us the previous year, she was familiar with the remarkable story so far. Nevertheless, she was surprised that I should take a dream so seriously. I was, by now, beginning to see that this was no ordinary dream, but a prophetic one. The full extent of its message would reveal itself in due course. Although not fully realising it at that time, the Lord was reviving the reason for my call to Ashland a year earlier.

A few moments later, the post arrived, and I was

absolutely shaken to find one of the letters was from south India, which was prominently stamped on the envelope! It was from the pastor whom I had met in Ashland, updating me on his progress and, at the same time, inviting me to visit the home, with a view to possibly gaining some financial support.

I had not heard from the pastor since shortly after we left Ashland and now the Lord had pre-warned me in a dream that perhaps the time was nearing when I would become involved with his mission. It had taken five years for us to meet between the Lord speaking to each of us in 1983 and our meeting in Ashland. I did not know it then, but it would take another year before our meeting in Madras would materialise, brought about by a set of coincidences, completely orchestrated by the Holy Spirit.

I did not respond to his invitation initially, partly because of the dream! I was so intimidated by it and terrified of finding myself stranded in India. This could well happen, as I knew from a past experience when I had to disembark and stay in Bangkok for three days whilst Tom had to fly the plane back to Sydney for a major repair.

Instead of waiting for the dream to reveal its message, my mind was racing ahead, and I was taking it too literally. Although I knew that dreams have only limited language, the language of symbols with which to speak, they can be quite specific at times. I would, however, need to wait until its symbolism became clearer. This would occur the following spring when Tom and I went for a second three-month posting to Sydney, during which time I attended a fortuitous weekend course on 'Dreams and Spirituality' at the Aquinas Academy in Sydney.

The Facilitator for the course was a Catholic nun, Psychologist and Spiritual Director. After introducing herself to the group, she threw out a question. What had attracted us to this course? Also, did anyone have a particular dream which they would like her to workshop with us. My hand shot up immediately and I was relieved at last to share my dream with a professionally trained person.

After listening carefully to every detail, the Facilitator commented that the dream could be interpreted on various levels, emotionally, spiritually, and psychologically, but her first comment was that this was a very typical mid-life dream. By this comment, she was referring to the analytical work of Psychologist, Carl Jung and his theory of the Anima and the Animus. Jung describes the Animus as the unconscious masculine side of a woman and the Anima as the unconscious feminine side of a man, each transcending the personal psyche.

In the distinctively gendered society in which I grew up, it would not have been thought appropriate for a woman to exhibit aggressive, assertive, or even perceived (masculine) behaviours, yet subconsciously these strengths are merely underdeveloped within the female. These hitherto unknown strengths within my psyche were being called forth in the dream. I was being called into an undertaking for which I felt totally inadequate or ill-equipped because of my present understanding of the roles of men and women. Yet my subconscious was drawing out these strengths. Likewise for men in such a society, it would not have been acceptable to show feminine traits such as sensitivity or gentleness. As Jung's theory goes, the development of these traits usually starts to emerge in mid-life, hence the Spiritual Director's opening comment about it being a typical mid-life dream. I was just approaching fifty at this time.

The symbolism of the fragile plane (representing my self-image/ego strength) compared pathetically with my image of Tom's capabilities because I knew in my conscious state that he flew the giant 747 Jumbo jet. In psychological terms, these underdeveloped strengths are in our shadow until such time as they are called forth. In the dream, there are words as well as symbols. Tom disappears, saying he cannot help me, and I would have to undertake this task alone, symbolised by the single seater plane.

As for the questions asked by me in the dream, "How will I navigate? Where will my refuelling stops be?" The reply, "Just head out!" was the spiritual aspect of the dream. It was a call to trust God. He would guide; He would be my source of power for what He was calling me to do, with the injunction, "Just head out!" This interpretation was most reassuring. The Lord had been faithful so far in leading me to this point; I felt sure that He would reveal the next step in due course.

As already mentioned, we were on a three-month posting in Sydney at the time, from February to May, and it was during this period that the Lord began to indicate the next move. One evening I was writing a letter to the children back home in England with the TV on quietly in the background when, suddenly, a thundering voice came from the TV-set screaming at the viewer, "INDIA - DO IT NOW!" I knew immediately that it was a message from the Lord, but I could not go until after our return to England. Besides which, we were expecting our son, Peter, to join us for the Easter holidays. On our return to England, I promised myself (or was it to the Lord?) that I would prepare to go to Madras.

A couple of weeks after this event, Peter arrived in Sydney, clutching in his hand the latest edition of *The British Airways News*, and on it, in bold capitals, on the front page, was the heading 'MADRAS ROUTE NOW OPENED.' With this headline, I could doubt no longer that I was indeed being called to India.

Once back home in England, the reality of what I was undertaking hit me forcefully. I had hoped Tom might be able to accompany me but after a three-month posting he had no holiday leave on which to draw and I heard the words he spoke in the dream echoing back, "I can't go with you, Pauline. You will have to go alone."

I was planning to travel early to mid-August, allowing sufficient time for the start of the first academic year of the two-year Pastoral Theology course I had just signed up for, when my plans were suddenly thwarted with the advent of the Gulf War, which started on 2nd August, closing the Madras route.

That is when the next piece of the puzzle fell into place, with a vision I had one evening at Mass. In this vision, I distinctly saw two suitcases, each with a pair of ladies' shoes beside them. What could this mean? As in previous times, I kept it in mind until it should reveal its meaning.

Quite out of the blue, I received a telephone call from Maureen, the Indian lady then living in London, whom I had met at the camp in Virginia. She told me she was travelling to Madras for a family wedding in the Autumn and thought she would like to look up the pastor who we had met in Ashland and asked if I would like to accompany her!

So, that was what the vision was about! The Lord was providing me with a companion. Not only that, but a way to get around the embargo on the Madras route brought about by the Gulf War. British Airways was still operating the Bombay route (something about not flying directly over a war zone), thus keeping this destination open, and, as Maureen quickly reassured me, if I were to fly to Bombay and meet her there, I could stay with her other son and his family and from there make plans for our onward journey together to Madras.

When I arrived in Bombay, I was met at the airport by Maureen and her son, who drove us to his family home in the smart coastal district of Bandra. By European standards, the home was quite simply furnished, though they seemed very proud of it. In comparison to the mere hovels, which the majority of people lived in, they could be justifiably proud. Primitive dwellings stretched from the airport perimeter right into the heart of the city.

One attractive feature of the son's house was that it had a rooftop garden, where the family could sit out in the cooler part of the day. Here, the family was waiting and had laid out for us some delicious food. It was when we were enjoying these delights that there suddenly erupted from the street below the noise of music from all kinds of instruments, singing and general merrymaking. Peering over the edge of the roof-top garden, I soon saw what all the noise was about; it was a wedding party escorting the Bride and Groom to their wedding ceremony.

Eventually, the noise of the wedding party faded, as they drifted away into the distance. Soon, Maureen was outlining the plans of how we were to travel to Madras. We would travel together by train, but her son, overhearing our plan would not hear of our travelling in such discomfort and even danger, (and if you ever saw an Indian train in transit, you would know why). People often cling tenaciously to the outside of carriages, with some even sitting on the train roof! No, he would quickly obtain two tickets for a flight to Madras. Again, fortuitously, he was a pilot for Air India and could pull some strings to bring this about.

When we arrived in Madras, I took a taxi to the mission. Maureen, meanwhile, met up with her other son and family, with a promise to meet up at the mission a day or two later.

As I stepped from the car at the mission, I was met like visiting royalty, receiving an overwhelming welcome from the pastor and his family, followed by a line-up of all the children in the home, who were introduced individually by name.

A girl of about eight who looked somehow poorer than the others, maybe because she was doing household duties at the time, was quickly invited to join the line-up and she, too, was introduced. Of all the children I met that day, she was the only one with an English name. My heart trembled in awe, as her name was announced - MARGARET. It was

Welcome Party India

at that moment when I knew this was where the Holy Spirit had been leading me.

During my week-long stay, I was shown the various activities of the children, at work and at play, and was really humbled to see how little they needed to entertain themselves. The boys had even encouraged a hen to play football. All the children were proud to show off their exercise routines and dancing skills. One little boy could even recite many long psalms by heart!

I was interested to learn the future plans for the mission. Money had already been raised in the USA for a church building to replace the primitive hut, which doubled as a church on Sundays and as a school room during the week.

The long-term plans were to build a mission centre. A church would be built to serve the people in the surrounding area. Then, when sufficient funds were raised, workshops would be built, where the children would learn weaving and carpentry, so that by the time the children left the home, they would be literate and would have a skill for life with which to support themselves. It would take time and funds

Children dancing
Madras

Hen playing football with boys
Madras

to achieve all of this, but they had tremendous faith that this would materialise.

This had been a long journey from that day in Yateley in 1983 and the vision of the white cow and the vision of the word 'India':

- to three times being called by my first name, Margaret in 1988 at the conference
- to the prophetic call to Ashland from Ruth
- and eventually meeting with the pastor from Madras in Ashland in 1988
- the dream of my being in 'south India' (1989)
- the TV commercial screaming out "India - do it now!" (1990)
- The British Airways newspaper headline 'Madras Route Now Opened' (1990)
- likewise, the 'Dreams and Spirituality' course in Sydney, in 1990
- the provision of a companion, (Maureen), promised by the vision of the two suitcases and two pairs of ladies' shoes

- overcoming the travel interruption caused by the Gulf War
- provision of accommodation in Bombay with Maureen's son - a pilot,
- and provision of concessionary flight tickets to Madras
- and finally, the pre-destined meeting with this little girl, Margaret!

All of this had been orchestrated by the Holy Spirit, free of charge! One of the names of God is Jehovah Jireh, which means 'The Lord provides.' He does indeed. Certainly, in all of these events, the Lord was in the detail!

After a couple of days, Maureen and her son and grandchildren from Madras joined us, and the children performed a concert in our honour. After spending a week at the mission, it was finally time to say goodbye and I had to make my return to Bombay to make the connection with the British Airways flight to London.

I had to fly back to Bombay alone, as Maureen stayed on with her family in Madras for the wedding.

At Bombay airport, a pleasant and surprising interlude occurred. I had checked in at the desk; my luggage had gone onto the conveyor belt, but I had an hour or two to wait for my flight to be called. I was probably looking a little lost and somewhat conspicuous as a lady travelling on my own, plus being the only European in sight, when I was approached by a most handsome, tall, Sikh gentleman. Having introduced himself with a most gracious bow, he invited me to follow him and his assistant to his reserved table, where coffee was offered to me from a tall coffee pot in a style typical in the Middle East and India. I assumed that he was booked on my flight, but after some time another internal flight, his flight, was called and once again he gave his gracious bow and was gone. It was a brief encounter I shall never forget.

On my return to Yateley, I was invited back to St Peters Church (where the first vision occurred), to share my story with its many twists and turns, emphasising how the Holy Spirit had led all the way.

As a result of my presentation, several people offered to support the mission financially and when I next visited Sydney to visit my daughter, a friend there, on hearing the tale, made a very generous donation of $800 which paid for a toilet block and other substantial buildings to replace the grass roofed lean-to buildings.

Unfortunately, it was not possible for me to provide adequate continuing oversight for the project as I had just started on a course in Pastoral Theology and besides, there was the possibility of another posting in the near future. But, it had all been an incredible missionary journey.

GOD'S GRACE ABOUNDS

WHERE TWO WORLDS CROSS
Sydney, May 1990

After spending a pleasant few days at the weekend residence of friend Lynne, approximately 45 miles north of Sydney, it was time to pack up and head back to the city.

The smell of fresh percolating coffee was drifting from the kitchen towards my bedroom, and along with it came the haunting melody of a tune which I did not recognise, but which drew my attention as if drawn to a magnet. The tune, I learned, was entitled *Be* from the film *Jonathan Livingston Seagull*.

On the way into the city, Lynne told me of her concern for a friend, Jan, whom she thought might have cancer, judging by the amount of weight she had lost since they last met, and the obvious pain she was suffering. She then surprised me by asking if I would visit her and pray for healing! Despite the fact that I had never claimed or even hinted at having a healing gift, she ignored my protestations to the contrary, urging me to see her anyway. I agreed to this proposition and promised to make contact as soon as possible.

Returning to the city, I made arrangements to see Jan, and was surprised to receive an invitation to meet up the following evening.

Not knowing what to expect from our meeting, I was shown into a consulting room, complete with examination couch, on which Jan beckoned me to make myself comfortable, meanwhile she settled herself on the only chair in the room. Once seated, she opened up with, "I believe you are about to return to England soon."

"Yes, unfortunately," came my immediate reply.

'Why unfortunately?"

"It's what it represents."

"And what is that?"

"Rejection."

What had prompted this emotional response was due to having only that day read the latest parish newsletter from home, which had stirred up memories of the unhappy times of feeling rejected when I spoke of the amazing experience of Baptism in the Holy Spirit.

Mentally, I was contrasting this feeling with the warm welcome we had received from the first day of our arrival in our parish in Sydney, even to the point of having been asked to join their Parish Council and being invited to speak about the Holy Spirit at several venues.

Before I realised it, I was in the skilful hands of a professional psychotherapist, trying to explain to her what I had been so woefully unable to convey to my parish priest and church friends, namely the tremendous blessing of Baptism in the Holy Spirit. It was this experience which I had struggled to describe to anyone who would listen, and having been misunderstood, I had come to feel un-affirmed and ostracised by most of my fellow parishioners. Sometime later, Father Carroll, the parish priest in Yateley, did eventually acknowledge that I had received what theologians call 'The Second Blessing.' Although it was good for my experience to be finally authenticated in this way, the initial rejection had obviously hurt me deeply.

It soon became clear that Jan was seeking to discover why it was so important for me to share my experience with others. Why not just keep it to myself since my attempts were being rejected? She was obviously looking to discern my motives. Was I just attention-seeking, desperate for approval and admiration? I have thought about a suitable reply to this question many times and on reflection, my best answer (though not original) is, "I'm just one beggar telling another beggar where he can find bread."[2] Put another way, "Let me show you what I've found. It will change your life."

"Tall Poppy Syndrome," I heard Jan half murmur to herself.

"Oh, what does that mean? I've not come across that expression before," I replied.

"It's an Australian term we use to describe how people are thwarted or criticised to effectively cut them down to size after they have been successful in some way."

I paused to take in what Jan had just said. It was not that I considered myself any better than anybody else. I merely wanted them to experience what I had, the life-changing, transforming power of the Holy Spirit. I had known

---

[2]   Quotes by D T Nile New York Times 1986

instinctively there was more to faith than I had so far experienced. Now, my horizons had been expanded; I was in a relationship with God through the power of the Holy Spirit and I wanted this for others too, but most people, it seemed, were simply content with the status quo.

Eventually, I felt like an outcast, but it was not the isolation so much as the refusal to learn something to their benefit which hurt the most. So, angrily, I had finally given up on them and began to associate more with other like-minded friends.

After a period of further skilful questioning, Jan finally put an important question to me. "In spite of all the rejection you have so obviously experienced, do you think you can forgive the 'flock' back home and try again to share what you have learned?"

How strange, I thought, to refer to my fellow parishioners in such a manner. But had not Jesus spoken of Himself and of His followers in just such terms?

"Do not be afraid little flock" (Luke 12:32)

"My sheep listen to My voice; I know them and they follow Me." (John 10:27)

"I am The Good Shepherd" (John 10:11)

With my carefully considered assent to Jan's question, she predicted a time when I would find one, possibly two or three people looking for guidance, ready to explore the still unchartered horizons of their spiritual existence, to go beyond the generally accepted norms. Once they grasped their own potential, they could become the person they were called to be. It just took belief that there were other possibilities and self-imposed limitations that could be overcome, from which a new, more fulfilling life would open up. With this change of outlook, they would become open to new ideas. What they could become would be in their grasp, as they, too, listened and believed the inner voice calling them onwards.

The questions went back and forth between us for quite some time until Jan, joining my hands together in a prayerful gesture, closed her own hands around mine, at the same time looking studiously into my face and saying, "Others may not have believed in you in the past, but I believe in you, Pauline." This was a true moment of grace, and the affirmation was both powerful and healing to my soul.

With that said, she took from her bag a trinket given to her on her wedding day, and placed it into my hands saying, "Whenever you doubt yourself or feel rejected, look at this and say, 'Jan believes in me.'" She then searched for something else, saying to herself. "Dash it, I've brought the wrong handbag with me today," and went on to explain what she meant by this.

Several weeks earlier, her Spiritual Director had given her a strange directive. She was to select a book from her library, which she was going to need for someone who would come into her life shortly. Visualising the hundreds of books which lined her study, floor to ceiling and wall to wall, Jan felt a little daunted by this task, until she was told exactly where she could locate the book in question. She was to go to the fifth shelf up and take from it the fourth book from the end, also indicating a relevant page on which the question posed was "Do you really want to fly?"

The book turned out to be one of the slimmest books in the whole library, entitled, *Jonathan Livingston Seagull* by Richard Bach (1970), a simple story of an ordinary seagull who spends all of his time challenging the usual limitations of a seagull, ignoring discouraging remarks from his flock.

Despite their comments, Jonathan flew purposefully on, attempting incredible speeds, and practising unimaginable dives and rolls. Undaunted, he pursued his quest. In so doing, he breaks through all the usual norms for a seagull, crashing through one limitation after another. For him, there was much more to life than merely scrabbling in the wake of a fishing boat for morsels of fish!

In spite of Jonathan's amazing flying achievements, he is eventually cast out, ostracised from the rest of the flock, destined to fly alone, far away, circling the high cliffs, until one day two dazzling white gulls, flying alongside him, matching manoeuvre for manoeuvre, spoke to him and took him under their wing (forgive the pun). They are gulls who, like himself, have progressed to new levels of flying. He learns even greater skills under their tutelage.

Surprising even to Jonathan himself, memories of those far off times when he was part of the flock came to mind. He had not thought about them for a long time and his achievements so far had benefitted no one but himself. Then, he is challenged to forgive the flock, rejoin them and work to help them learn.

Now, that same challenge was being put to me. Since being given the instruction about the book, Jan had carried it around in her handbag each day, waiting for another 'Jonathan' type to cross her path. In listening to my story, she could see clear parallels with the book's theme and my history. Not only that, but she saw how our two lives had paralleled, "in ways you will never know," she commented. Now, at last, fate (or The Holy Spirit) had arranged this meeting and our two lives had finally crossed. "Our meeting had been inevitable," she murmured, quoting a line oft quoted by the famous poet T S Eliot, "at the point of intersection."

Jan then spoke a little about her present circumstances. She did have a serious illness, which caused her much pain. The previous night, she had been in so much discomfort she rose early, taking her little dog for its daily walk along the beach. The sun was just coming up, like a huge golden orb in the sky, and Jan had cried out, "God, please help me."

That very morning, Lynne had called in to see if I had made contact with Jan yet, which is how I was given an immediate appointment for that evening. Jan had worked through the rest of the day, despite her discomfort, and by the time evening came and our appointment was due, she really did not feel up to keeping it, but agreed to see me anyway.

What she said next would take my breath away. She had suffered pain all day and really wanted nothing more than to go home to rest. "But," she said, "from the moment you arrived, I have been totally free from pain." It would appear that our meeting had produced healing in the other, as our lives intersected.

"And another thing, ever since you came in, I have been drawn to your wedding ring. Look at mine, they are identical, yet another indication of how our lives have paralleled, even to that detail." How amazing is that? Jan's ring was bought in Manly, Australia, whilst mine was bought in Manchester, England. At the time our rings were bought, wedding rings were usually a plain narrow band, but ours were wider, with a very distinctive engraved pattern.

When Lynne and I met up the next day, she was holding in her hand a copy of *Jonathan Livingston Seagull,* which she had bought for me, even before I had a chance to share the startling conversation with Jan the evening before! Lynne's handwritten dedication inside the cover reads as follows:

'May the thought in playing the tape this morning, BE in total recognition of the Holy Spirit's influence to gain from His wisdom.'

I had one more meeting with Jan before returning to England and kept in touch for a little while, long enough for her to learn of my change of fortune, as she had predicted. Within six months from our meeting, I had been invited to join a new Pastoral Theology course for lay people, introduced by the Vatican, after which I set up and taught a small group of potential leaders in the parish, one of whom later became a Deacon. At a retreat a little later, I met the Diocesan Director of Education who, hearing of my studies, invited me to join the Diocesan team. Further opportunities led to a five-year study to become a counsellor/

psychotherapist, again unconsciously mirroring my soul-mate, Jan, in Australia. Our conversation that fateful, healing evening had set the wheels in motion for me to become all that I had been called to BE.

> *"In Every Moment of Time, you live*
> *Where Two Worlds Cross." (T S Eliot)*

RESCUE ON THE M3
December 1991

As we neared the end of the first term of my second year of the Pastoral Theology course, Theology Tutor Father John Farrell, invited us to the *Pastoral Review*, a variety show held each year by the priests of the Southwark diocese. It promised to be an entertaining evening, and I looked forward to seeing Father John in a completely different role. He was always a good sport in class, and invariably our lessons were punctuated by his raucous laughter, which, of course, was infectious. Despite this, and most probably because of his humour, he trained us to think philosophically and theologically, guiding us through some very difficult theological concepts.

As time came round for the review, Tom and I invited our friend, Vernon, to accompany us. On the day, we set off in good time for the show but, unfortunately, we never arrived, due to a near fatal accident. As I recall it, the traffic was moving rather slowly so Tom had moved into the outer lane. After a short while, another car suddenly cut directly in front of us, leaving no space to manoeuvre. Before we knew it, we had crashed into the central barrier, which started us on a series of spins right across the other lanes of traffic.

As we started to spin, I found myself calling out from my position in the back seat, "Jesus, help us, Jesus, help us!" Still the spinning continued until, quite miraculously, we came to what seemed like a planned halt on the hard shoulder! Tom was an excellent and competent driver, but this escape from death was beyond even his skilful driving. It was as if we had been lifted out of the traffic by unseen hands and placed down safely out of harm's way.

We did not have mobile phones in those days to summon help, but another driver had spotted what had happened and called for help on our behalf at the next emergency telephone box, so we were more than a little surprised when the AA arrived a short time later. The mechanic announced that the car was not able to be driven, and had to be towed away. How then, had Tom managed to steer us to safety? Or had divine help indeed intervened?

We were driven from the scene by taxi. When we arrived home and were sitting around the kitchen table, we pondered on what had just happened. We talk of some things being a miracle, which is purely hyperbole, a form of extreme exaggeration to make a strong impact, however, Vernon was quite certain it was a miracle, from his vantage point in the front seat.

At some point in our discussion, I said I thought we should have a Mass of Thanksgiving said for our survival.

The very next day, at Mass the reading of certain verses, taken from Psalm 116 jumped out at me and we knew we had indeed been rescued from death on the M3. Below are some of the relevant verses.

How can I repay the Lord for all His goodness to me?
I will lift up the cup of salvation and call on the name
of the Lord.
I will fulfil my vows to the Lord in the presence of all
His people.
(Berean Standard Bible Psalm 116: 12-13)

AN UNUSUAL REQUEST
August 1996

Never say, "No" if you can say, "Yes." This has long since been one of my mottoes for life, so when Gemma's request came one Saturday morning, I automatically replied in this manner, only to realise later the enormous challenge my automatic, "Yes" would present.

The request started simply enough. Would I follow up a call from a headmistress whose school was closing; she had some items we might be interested in for a charity we were supporting in south-east Nigeria called The Voice of the Poor. Gemma was definitely interested, but was due to go to Ireland on a speaking engagement, so would I follow this up and let her know the outcome?

Monday morning came and I rang the school. To my query, "Which items may we have from the school," thinking maybe a few dozen reading books and possibly maths books, too, the Head replied, "You can have the lot." The whole school was ours for the taking!

That evening, Gemma phoned to catch up on the conversation. Relaying the exact words that were spoken, there came a very short pause, then Gemma said, "Tell her we'll take the lot!" When I conveyed this information to the Head, she only then mentioned a proviso. We had to clear out the school within two weeks!

Gemma then asked me, "Pauline, another request, do you think you and Tom could handle this project for me?"

"Of course," I found myself replying, in my usual cooperative manner, only at that moment beginning to realise the enormity of the task that I had committed us to.

The next day, when Tom and I visited the school and were shown its contents, we realised we needed a team of helpers. A quick call to several friends, three of whom were teachers, so had an interest in the project, led to them signing up immediately to help. Others joined in and got to grips with the logistics of heaving and hauling heavy items, such as several hundred books, pupils' desks, teachers' desks, chairs, cupboards, computers, laboratory equipment, blackboards, whiteboards, percussion instruments, kitchen items, sports equipment, netball posts, even dressing up clothes and Christmas items!

The team sprang into action immediately, even before Gemma left. Before long, we were working like a well-oiled machine. Tom and son, Stephen made many journeys to Gemma's house, car loaded to capacity, with smaller items packed up in boxes.

Meanwhile, one of the helpers who owned a fencing company, made numerous journeys to Gemma's place with larger items. These were unloaded and stored in various garages belonging to friends, until such time as funds could be raised to ship the items to Nigeria. The shipping company would pick up the items from Gemma's house in due course.

On these trips, Gemma, a Canadian by birth, had pancakes, generously spread with maple syrup, while waiting for the helpers to enjoy an impromptu breakfast or mid-morning break.

The enormity of the work involved was daunting, to say the least, yet using our various skills, goodwill and plenty of good humour, the task was completed in record time!

The next phase of the project was to raise funds to ship the items to Nigeria in containers. In the meantime, all the items were stored in various homes and garages around Ascot until the shippers collected them to be stored 'temporarily' at their work site, before being loaded, item by item, in the presence of an inspector, at a later date.

I was present on more than one occasion when Gemma had to sweet-talk staff from the container company, who were running out of space at their work site with no fixed date to complete the shipment, while funding for the shipment was being sourced. The staff were terrific and even helped us compact various items and find additional storage, in their own time. Eventually, the day arrived when sufficient funds were raised, and we said farewell to the items and bid them 'bon voyage.'

The next we heard about the shipment was that it had arrived safely and was being stored on the wharf until being collected. This was the point at which pilfering might occur, but not a single item was missing from our shipping lists - not even a screw!

Another wonderful thing happened when the goods arrived. Somebody noticed on the shipping list that there were items suitable for Christmas - two Christmas trees and a full set of tree decorations. There was a chest freezer, an item which no one had seen before! These items were quickly unpacked and sent on ahead so that they might be put to use in time for the festive season.

The items arrived early Christmas Eve and by the time Midnight Mass was to be celebrated, the two Christmas trees, by now fully decorated, stood proudly either side of the sanctuary, giving such obvious pleasure to everyone at Mass, but especially the children.

Yet another surprise was in store the next day. Overnight, the freezer had been plugged in to freeze water and the congregation was able to experience ice for the very first time.

We were overjoyed to hear this feedback after all our efforts, but greater fruits were to come from this first initiative. In later years, another project I was actively engaged in was to collect walking sticks and wheelchairs from the British Red Cross. In addition, each week, the Superintendent of the community centre where I worked as a volunteer, providing lunches for the members of the Multiple Sclerosis Club, gave me clothing and shoes. A donation of hospital beds and other medical items from a local hospital also followed.

The motto of this reflection? Never say, "No" - you don't know what possibilities may result or where it will lead you!

WALKING STICKS AND
WHEELCHAIRS
Winchester 1998

Whenever I hear a request from my very good friend Gemma, it is usually a little out of the ordinary to say the least. This time was no exception. Would Tom and I travel to the main storage depot of the British Red Cross in Winchester to pick up a selection of second-hand wheelchairs to send to the charity we were supporting in Nigeria. The one mentioned in the last chapter. Another friend would meet up with us to load the items onto his lorry; he would then take them to yet another friend who could overhaul and re-commission them before shipping.

We gasped as we entered the storage depot. It was huge, with disability aids of all kinds stacked from floor to ceiling. The staff was expecting us and started immediately to select a number of wheelchairs, which had been taken down from their stacked position, and carried them near to the door. 'Mission accomplished' I thought but not quite yet; they then brought down several commodes and placed them with the wheelchairs.

"What about walking sticks?" asked one of the men and with that a dozen or so were placed alongside our growing pile. We looked a little cautiously at all the items, wondering how just Tom and I could manage, but assistance was offered by the staff, on the condition that we took them before five o'clock when they finished for the day.

Gemma had told us that someone would turn up with a lorry (no description, name or logo given with which to identify it) and, although the driver had never met us before, somehow we would recognise each other! Recognition would not be difficult for the driver, as Tom and I each sat conspicuously at the end of a row of wheelchairs and commodes! But there was a slight hitch, we might have to stay at our posts for up to two hours because the driver could not get there until sometime between six and seven o'clock (These were the days before mobile phones were common so we had no means of contacting each other).

There was nothing else to do but make use of the assistance offered by the depot staff to get the items into the street. What a sight we must have made for the workers hurriedly piling out of the nearby offices! Thank goodness our English weather held out as we sat in the cold for nearly two hours, but at least it was dry!

Time passed slowly but, eventually, an old lorry rattled by and spotted us. Soon, the various items for Nigeria were loaded onto it and our small contribution to the overall effort was complete. Happily, that was not the end of the story from our perspective.

Many years later, I heard of a long-term outcome from that shipment of wheelchairs, one of which was a child's one. That small wheelchair was immediately given to a young disabled boy, unable to walk as a result of having had polio and whose parents were unable to care for him. He had been taken in by Rev. Msgr. John Bosco Akam and the growing community, and brought up by them. This boy turned out to be very bright and completed primary and secondary schooling with relish. He was the first of a number of disabled people to complete a university degree at the Tansian University, founded in Umunya, in 2009.

The blessings have continued. In 2016, Gemma and her husband, Ian, returned from visiting Nigeria and attending the graduation of the once-young-boy who had received the small wheelchair. Some of us, who had been involved in sending out the containers met to see photos and hear about how the various projects were going. The now-young-man and some of the others from this community are now employed at the university.

We gave thanks for all that had been accomplished by the Lord through our simple, "Yes."

A DIFFERENT KIND OF JOURNEY

FOR BETTER FOR WORSE
March 2000

"You know he'll never be the same again, don't you?" These were the words I least needed to hear from a nursing friend of ours, when she heard the extent of Tom's stroke.

I did not want to acknowledge the fact to myself, even after I saw him for the first time on the ward after being in ICU for the first few days, but I could not deny the reality of the statement when I first saw him. Gone were the strikingly handsome features I had known and admired for so many years. In their place a different face stared back at me - a frightened look in his eyes and an awful, lop-sided twist to his mouth, distorting his appearance almost beyond recognition. Even his hair appeared to be standing on end, as if he had received an electric shock.

Indeed, he had received a shock. What must it have been like for him to gain consciousness only to find he was paralysed on one side and could no longer speak? It must have been terrifying! Was this truly his fate, permanently? Fear gripped my whole body at this thought. News of our circumstances swiftly passed around our church community and many prayers, both communally and privately were prayed.

A week on the Stroke Ward and a series of tests later confirmed that Tom had just scraped through with sufficient points to gain a place at the specialist Stroke Unit at Farnham Hospital where he could receive physio and speech therapy.

Hopes were raised with this news and once he was transferred to Farnham, they were raised even more when I saw some patients making a degree of improvement. Meanwhile, I attended every physio and speech session.

Our Agony in the Garden

Sadly, despite all the dedicated professional treatment and the hours I spent at his bedside exercising his arm, to encourage and stimulate muscle memory, there was no response on any front, which was most discouraging. What would the future hold for Tom, for us, as we dealt with the aftermath of the calamity which had struck both our lives?

I remember Eastertime very clearly that year, falling as it did just a month or so after the stroke. Throughout our married life, Easter usually would have found us in church following the account of The Passion (Sufferings) of Jesus, as recorded in various Gospels.

That year, I shared the Easter readings with Tom, at his bedside. Never had the readings seemed so poignant and relevant to our situation, especially the scene where Jesus, seeing what lay before Him, cried out in prayer to His Father in the Garden of Gethsemane the night before He died.

"My Father, if it is possible,
may this cup be taken from Me.
Yet not as I will but as You will."
(Matthew 26:39).

It would take time and grace to be able to say the second part of this prayer with any degree of honesty. I just wanted my husband well again and our nice, cosy comfortable life back!

Coming to Terms

Slowly, I began to come to terms with the impact of the stroke and looked for any signs of change. At the suggestion of the Speech Therapist, I experimented with all sorts of trigger-inducing responses, such as reciting the alphabet and calling out well known phrases, hoping to jolt his brain into completing the expression. Another suggestion was to count numbers, hoping to trigger memory and an automatic response to the rhythm of the counting. Yet another suggestion was to recite familiar poems, nursery rhymes and prayers - all things learned early in life and which had formed deep pathways or memories. Still no response.

I followed the Speech Therapist's instructions to encourage Tom to form his mouth to make appropriate speech sounds and when he eventually came home from hospital, we purchased a computer-based aid called "Speech Sounds on Cue" to continue this form of therapy. We also engaged in a university trial, which hopefully would provide an electronic voice for Tom's touchscreen input. Regrettably, our efforts with these devices were totally futile, as Tom had lost the ability to sequence information and to remember pathways. Eventually, the day came when I was told that Tom's speech would probably never return!

At the thought of this, the colour drained from my face like the sea withdrawing from the land at the turn of the tide.

My Grace is Sufficient for You

The devastating news about Tom's speech was absolutely shocking, and it broke my heart! I entered a period of deep mourning on Tom's behalf, though I could not show my feelings in front of him. Always, he must travel in hope!

We naturally explored all the usual avenues for healing such as the Sacrament of the Sick, taking Tom to Lourdes and having Deacon Pat Taylor pray with him for healing several times. Disappointingly, none of these pursuits produced any significant change. It was particularly disappointing as I had witnessed so many other healings through Deacon Pat's healing ministry including that of close friends.

We had run out of options and were starting to feel despondent, similar to how St Paul must have felt after praying to the Lord three times for a sickness or illness to be removed. Just as the Lord had replied to St Paul, "My grace is sufficient for you," maybe I, too, had to take on board this response for myself and carry it forward in all that life was to bring my way.

"My grace is sufficient for you,
for my power is made perfect in weakness"
(2 Corinthians 12:9).

A New Dawn Emerges

At this time, I was in my final year of Counselling Training and just about to be assessed once I had completed one hundred hours of client work. So far, I had completed seventy-six client hours, more than all my fellow trainee counsellors because I had been fortunate in finding a placement in which to work much earlier than they had.

As soon as my trainers heard about Tom and could see how deeply affected I was, they instantly cancelled any contact with clients, "for at least a year" to allow me to recover from such a significant loss. One or two of my cohort had still not even found a placement at that stage, so a decision was made to extend the course for another year to allow everyone the opportunity to complete it. This was an unexpected turn of events and worked to my advantage, allowing me at least the satisfaction and sense of fulfilment in finally qualifying. Meanwhile, Tom's condition showed no improvement.

On one occasion, the physios introduced Tom to an electric wheelchair, but this was quickly withdrawn when it became apparent that his vision was affected. He had what is described as 'right-sided neglect.' Anyone walking along the corridor when Tom was around ran the risk of being knocked down because he only saw one side. It was the same with reading. Tom still had some level of reading skill, but he failed to read the whole line because of this impairment.

It is quite natural to assume that Tom could communicate by writing, but even this was beyond his capabilities. The only thing he ever managed to write was his signature (which obviously had deep pathways in his brain). He even wrote a scrawled version of his formal signature (T J Doyle) rather than his usual birthday card signature of 'Tommy' on a birthday card to me, which I still treasure to this day.

At some stage, we bought a board and magnetic letters for him to spell out words, but he could not pick out the letters in the correct sequence. It would appear that all means of communicating were denied him. How stranded and lost he must have felt!

A little more reassurance came when, one day in physio, it was noticed that he was able to put a little weight through his affected knee. Within a few weeks, he was able to stand, and with that came the hope that he might walk again. Hopeful news at last! By the time he was discharged from hospital at the end of four and a half months, he could walk falteringly with the aid of a special three-pronged walking stick. Physio continued at home and, eventually, Tom could climb the stairs and once more was able to sleep in his own bed.

For Better for Worse, In Sickness and in Health

Once Tom was home from hospital, we were introduced to the Stroke Club, a weekly support group for stroke patients. On our first attendance, I met some of the wives of other stroke patients (not 'victims' as we sometimes fell into the habit of saying) and joined them for coffee and mutual support. Another shock awaited me there, because although the conversation was sometimes about positive matters such as a medical breakthrough, it was mostly about reporting their present difficulties, frustrations and disappointments.

What struck me with full force the first time I met up with them, was to hear how long some of them had been caring for their husbands, with little hope of change. One long term carer had been doing so for twelve years, others for less long, but significant lengths of time all the same. How do they keep going I thought, as a shudder went through me, thinking that I, too, could share the same fate?

Life became a seesaw. We would experience a breakthrough, such as climbing the stairs and gaining access to the bathroom and bedroom, and for weeks we would live in equilibrium. Then, unsuspectingly, a setback would occur. For instance, one evening as we were having dinner, Tom's arm suddenly flung across the table, sending his dessert crashing onto the floor. He had just experienced his first stroke-induced seizure, and life was changed forever in that moment.

The fallout from the seizure made it impossible for Tom to climb stairs for fear of having another one whilst attempting this feat. It was not even to be considered, let alone attempted, until he had been seizure free for three months!

Thus began a period of hoping and praying for his stability. We would begin crossing off the weeks on the calendar. One, maybe three weeks would go by and hopes were raised, but another attack would send us back to square one again. Five, seven, even nine weeks went by in one counting period and we were really hopeful, then it happened again. Back to week one again! It was so demoralising and difficult to keep our hopes raised.

Finally, the elusive target was achieved and spirits were flying high, until one day, just as Tom was about to take the final step onto the landing at the top of the stairs, his legs suddenly buckled and I somehow managed to catch his crumbling body across my shoulders, as I followed from behind. Fortunately, I do not tend to panic in alarming situations, but am able to pause, consider the predicament and work out my best strategy. This is how I coped in this situation. With an almighty heave I somehow projected Tom safely onto the landing and he was safe! Thank God!

As soon as the physio heard of this episode, the decision was taken out of our hands. Tom must never attempt the stairs again. Another door to recovery and normality had been closed forever.

With this development, a hospital bed was set up in the living room, with another single bed alongside for me. The lounge thus became a virtual prison, functioning for all of Tom's needs for the next four years, until my eventual decision to build a custom-built extension.

In the meantime, in an attempt to give Tom some degree of autonomy, tests were carried out to see if he could become more independent in terms of personal hygiene and feeding himself. Alas, he was diagnosed with dyspraxia, a condition that affects the way the brain processes information, producing difficulty with coordination and manifesting in various, sometimes amusing ways, such as attempting to eat soup using a fork, or brushing his hair with his toothbrush, even washing his face without water! This bizarre behaviour, I was told, has nothing to do with intelligence.

Even comprehension is affected. Although he could not speak, speech itself could be understood if given time to process it. Often people did not realise this and on many occasions his attempt to converse was dismissed or over-looked with embarrassment. It pained me to see Tom so diminished and easily dismissed, especially their overlook-ing the man behind the disability. It was not their fault; they never knew Tom in his former life, but I wanted to scream, "This man used to fly Jumbo Jets!"

It may have been at this point, after so little had been achieved despite sheer hard work and determination on both our parts, that an even worse situation began to surface - anger - one of the stages of the grieving process. This would display itself in various forms - reaching out in the car to take the steering wheel out of my hands whilst driving or refusing to cooperate in helping him to get out of the car at the end of a journey. It was the only way Tom could exercise power or give him any sense of control. Even-tually I, not Tom, was referred to a psychologist, to train me how to manage such potentially dangerous situations and how to protect myself from him striking out at me. I had never anticipated such a change in his personality - another learning curve to negotiate!

Fortuitously, my counselling training came to the fore

at this stage, in helping me to understand to some extent what Tom was experiencing in terms of frustration, thus allowing me to offer the very necessary encouragement, patience and compassion he so desperately needed.

But I had needs too and these had largely been over-looked for too long. Since qualifying as a counsellor, I had not yet resumed contact with clients and could not see how I might achieve this, without help in terms of respite from caring for Tom. Technically, respite was provided for the client, not the carer, so there seemed no way around this, but sometime later new legislation was introduced, stating that a carer was entitled to some respite in his/her own right. After much form filling and many telephone conversations, I was granted ten hours respite per week, which I quickly earmarked and used for client hours!

Adjacent to where my counselling agency was situated, a new facility opened up called 'Disability Initiative' - the ideal place for Tom to meet other people and to explore his present capabilities. It was a perfect match for both our needs, or so it seemed, until the day came when Tom took on one of his stubborn moods and refused to get out of the car. After coaxing and cajoling him for ten minutes or so and knowing that the time with my client was fast approaching, I sought help from the disability team. We were lucky that first time, but soon his refusal to cooperate became a pattern. Tom was making a very firm statement.

When I told the agency, they said it was unethical for me to continue to practise when I was under so much strain, but if I made other satisfactory arrangements for Tom and wished to return, I would be welcome. With that, another door closed, for a time.

True Grit and Determination

Another episode when Tom refused to get out of the car, and which encapsulates both the anxiety and humour which can come from a potentially extremely dangerous situation readily comes to mind. We had just returned from a journey when Tom stubbornly refused to get out of the car. It had been another failed attempt to find out where Tom wanted to go. We were beginning to realise that Tom's orientation skills were returning and, with the point of a finger right, left or straight ahead, we were often successful in discovering the required destination. Not so on this occasion, and I had finally given up the attempt, raising Tom's anger to boiling point.

The psychologist had trained me to leave him alone in the car, for a short period, then to return to see if he had calmed down. This was also to teach him that, although I appeared to have abandoned him, like any good mother will tell you, a child only learns trust by being left. It was a fact that 'mother' always returns. It was the only way to teach dependability. I had to use these simple skills now to allow for Tom's anger to abate. Each time I left him, I had to extend the time before returning.

My concern was that he might get out of the car and fall, but the psychologist and physio both assured me that because of his paralysis, this was not possible.

It was on one of these occasions, when I was anxiously

counting how long it had been since I left him, that I was shocked to the core on hearing his voice right behind me! To this day I cannot figure out how he managed to get out of the car safely, walk along eight feet of patio alongside the house, turn round the corner and climb two steps into the house before letting out an almighty roar of pure fury! So much for the training manuals on safe conduct for carers. Tom had just made a case for it to be re-written!

Another somewhat amusing episode occurred in hospital, following a time of re-admittance for recuperation and rehab, after suffering from pneumonia and a nasty bug called Clostridium Difficile at the same time. Either one of these conditions can cause death, but despite these and Tom's other 'morbidities' he still had a strong constitution and survived. Unfortunately, during this time he again lost his ability to walk and was discharged with the comment "No rehab potential." Life's seesaw had gone down once again. But, we never took into consideration Tom's enormous resilience and determination.

For days Tom had indicated that he wanted me to take him somewhere and kept pointing to his body. It was often simpler and quicker to reduce his frustration by getting into the car and allowing him to point to where he wanted to go, which I did on this occasion. Following his directions he led me straight back to the hospital, over five miles away! Honouring his attempts to communicate, I asked him if his gestures to his body was about physio. A vigorous nod of the head left me in no doubt what his wishes were, so I made enquires to see if the physio was in that day.

As luck would have it, she was, and when I explained what was going on, she invited me to take him to the gym, there and then, "to see what he can do" because, as she explained, "he always did better when you were around." (I think this was merely a communication issue, with which I was more familiar).

Once inside the gym, the physio took him to a bar to practice sitting to standing, which he negotiated well. She was about to bring the session to a close when Tom pointed to the parallel bars. "You don't think he wants to try them, do you?" she murmured under her breath. "That's exactly what he is saying," I replied, wondering what her reaction would be. "Well, let's give him a chance," and with that she wheeled him to the bars.

You must remember, Tom had only one usable arm with which to grab the rail. Pulling himself into an upright position, the physio was about to give him some reassuring instruction about following behind with the wheelchair, when he started walking, made it to the end, then negotiated a turn and made his return! Everyone was flabbergasted. What an amazing man! Scrapped were the "No rehab potential" notes, and, at my request, we had a bar fitted in our kitchen, which had a right-hand turn to negotiate round the corner. For fun, we used to put a little sweet at the end of the run, as a treat for his hard work. There were smiles as well as tears in those days.

My Love, My Life
Fast forward a few more years and another period in

hospital later, again the hard work gained in terms of mobility had been lost. Tom had also lost weight dramatically during another spell of pneumonia, after which he developed a condition called 'dysphagia', a swallowing problem. His swallow reflex had been compromised ever since the stroke, but became noticeably worse at this stage, and could be frightening both for patient and carer. It was at this stage that our GP first hinted that Tom may need to be fed by a feeding tube in his stomach, for safety reasons.

It may also have been at this suggestion that I added yet another request to my prayer list concerning Tom's welfare. So far, I had requested that I may live long enough to care for him to the end; that he may never need to go into a nursing home; that I may always be able to manage all the nursing skills required in caring for him and now I added that he may never need a feeding tube.

Eventually, however, it was suggested that Tom should go into a nursing home, because his nursing needs were "too complex for one person to manage and besides, you are still relatively young and need your own life."

Alas, they did not understand my commitment. "But he **is** my life," I replied, "and if you feel I need help to nurse him, then please help me to obtain it."

Roses in December

The prospect of Tom having to go into a care home set my mind drifting to our journey to date and how far we had come together.

Tom had come into my life while we were still in our

teen years. I had only shed my school uniform a matter of a few months earlier, at the tender age of seventeen, when I was invited by his sister to make up a foursome on Tom's final weekend after a short spell of leave in England, before returning to Germany where he was based in the RAF. Although only a mere two years older than me, he seemed so mature to me, having been exposed to life in the wider world. It was natural, therefore, for me to look up to him in recognition of his greater experience.

So, our first rendezvous was a blind date, (we had not met before), and over the years, when recalling this fact, I used to say, jokingly, "and if I had had both eyes wide open, I could not have chosen better!" He was very tall and extremely handsome, his skin flushed with a gentle tan from living on an island, and a smile which would light up a room. It was love at first sight, and as I learned subsequently, the feeling was mutual.

The test of our love was proven and justified by the long and patient courtship before our marriage four years later. Most of our courtship was conducted through frequent letters to each other, which became the highlight of the week for each of us.

During Tom's years in the Air Force, he became skilled as a maintenance engineer, but he had his sights set on a career in flying. When he was twenty, he came back to England to go through aptitude tests for this. The result was both positive in that he had passed the aptitude tests but disappointing in that the examiners decided to turn down his application on that occasion, advising him in the meantime to "lose your northern accent, then apply again." He was appalled at this comment, considering it something of an insult and never applied again on principle! Another of his qualities, he was a principled man.

Despite this setback, he never lost sight of his dream to fly, which he clung onto tenaciously. When he finally left the RAF, and even when we had a young family, he somehow managed to balance work, study at college and the duties of a young husband and father, until at last his newly gained qualifications enabled him to apply to train as a Flight Engineer, eventually gaining a position with BOAC, later to morph into British Airways.

All of his hard work and determination paid off handsomely, in providing the family with a more than privileged lifestyle in the form of exotic holidays and other travel opportunities.

And it gave him an obvious amount of pleasure to take us to some of the most beautiful places he had visited on trips. In fact, the family was never far from his thoughts wherever he flew and he often returned home with baskets of fruit from Nairobi, beautiful bed linens and tablecloths from India, orchids from Bangkok, Christmas tableware from New York and gadgets for the home from Macey's in New York. Yes, he was a gadget man, sometimes displaying his mischievous sense of fun, such as when he bought a fly-swatting gun! It was obvious that we were never far from his thoughts.

Tom was naturally away from home for very long periods. These were sometimes lonely times for me and challenging too, as I struggled to be both Mum and Dad in Tom's absence. And if ever anything were to go wrong with either the children or the home, it would surely happen the moment he was away.

Despite these setbacks, I was completely supportive of him and his chosen career (even though I was fearful of flying) and I was filled with pride as I waved him off each time, looking as dashing as ever in his uniform.

My reverie drifted further to more recent times, to our lives after Tom's stroke. We had good times too.

I started to recollect about how fiercely I had resisted the suggestion of him going into a care home, when he first had his stroke (after all he was only sixty-two) and how I had fought tooth and nail to get an adequate care package. In fact, because Tom's care needs were so complex and he needed two people to hoist him, the live-in carer was also supported by day-time carers for personal care etc. The additional care was very welcome and whilst having someone (quite often a complete stranger) living in your own home round the clock was a huge intrusion into our privacy, some of the carers became dear and trusted friends.

Usually, the live-in carers stayed for a couple of weeks then were relieved by another carer but one particular carer, Rose, chose not to adopt the usual work pattern and sometimes stayed for more than a month at a time. Rose became as close as family to us and I welcomed both the compassionate care she gave to Tom and the companionship we shared. She was deeply religious and I welcomed her Christian fellowship.

Further memories came flooding back of some of the daytime carers who brought such joy into our lives, each with their unique brand of humour and ways of engaging with Tom. There was 'Irish Mary' as we called her, who took delight in calling him 'The Doyle' and used to tease him on Sundays if we were going to church that day. Ever the evangelist, Tom would indicate 'Of course' then point to her as if to say, "And what about you?" Unfortunately, her duties did not permit this, but this banter went on between them, until at last Mary agreed to attend Mass on her next Sunday off.

Then there was Joan, a fellow northerner from Bury, which we used to pronounce as the locals from Bury pronounce the name, which brought a round of giggles. We felt at home with her from the word go and we followed each other's families with interest.

Brigitte supported us for many years and accompanied us on two cruise holidays, as did Bob on one occasion on a river cruise. He was a welcome change for Tom as they could 'talk' man to man as they say.

My namesake, Pauline brought her calming presence and prevented many a potentially difficult situation from escalating. On the plus side, we shared many happy hours at Costa Coffee and other venues.

Support from the parish took many different forms, of special note in times of sickness, was when Holy Communion was brought to us at home and the Union of Catholic Mothers (UCM) paid for our trip to Lourdes. Support came, too, from many individuals in the parish and from other friends.

Tom's stroke had been hard for the whole family to come to terms with and we all had to adjust. Our three children grieved for their lost father, who had always been there to help them with their cars, put up curtain poles or just go for an impromptu pint.

Tom engaging with his grandchildren 2002

The grandchildren had to get used to a 'new Grandad' no longer able to join in rough and tumble with them or chase them round the room. Tom had loved being with the grandchildren and in fact, it was the sound of the grandchildren's voices which brought him round to full consciousness and recognition of anything or anyone when he was first in hospital.

Obviously, it was very hard for Tom, too, and he made a monumental effort to keep that special relationship alive in any way he could.

Despite all of that, we had many years of good family life, and Tom was always at the heart of it.

His brothers, Leo and Bernard and his sisters, Anne and Mary came to visit when he was ill but also to celebrate the special birthdays and anniversaries. Mary even flew over from Australia on more than one occasion.

We found new ways of all being together or doing things

as a family - pub lunches, cinema and theatre trips, family parties, barbecues and the like. We always tried to find a way of getting Grandad's wheelchair in! What's more, it taught us all a huge lesson in patience,

Tom and Pauline celebrating Golden Wedding with Anne, Peter and Stephen

compassion and respect and that true love endures no matter how difficult the circumstances.

From time to time, people would comment on the respect I showed Tom in social situations, for instance in the discussion groups held in our home, when Tom would give an input. Clearly, his speech was merely a garble of sounds but I knew he was making a point and wanted this to be considered so I tried to give a voice to his thoughts.

Sometimes, my suggestion was so wide of the mark, he would burst into laughter, as if to say, "That's nothing like what I'm trying to say at all." On these occasions, we would all share in the joke and I would try again.

The technique I used to draw out the essence of what he was trying to say was to ask him tentatively, "Tom, are you saying something like … (such and such)" to which he would nod his head as in an excited "Yes" much to the astonishment of the group. This attunement on my part came from many years of spending time together and listening to each other's point of view.

Another aspect that people commented on was "the incredible patience" I showed. This stemmed from the deep compassion I felt for Tom in his predicament, the silent world, in which he was otherwise trapped.

Although I did my utmost to relieve this, I often felt more relief when he was asleep, knowing that then he was unaware. At moments like this, I would often look into his sleeping countenance and wonder "Why, God, did Tom have to suffer like this?"

Over time, the reason gradually dawned on me. I realised that the answer was to be found in the transformation occurring in my own character, indeed my whole being. The quality of my love in those moments was of a kind previously unawakened in me and our level of intimacy one previously unknown.

Some of the most difficult times had become some of the most precious to me and that promise of sufficient grace, ("My grace is sufficient for you") had come to fruition.

What an honour and privilege it was to care for Tom and what a blessing it is to have such rich memories!

"God gave us memory so that we might have
roses in December" - J. M. Barrie

LOURDES REVISITED
September 2002

Following Tom's stroke, many kindnesses were shown to us. I have already mentioned that one of these was from The Union of Catholic Mothers (UCM). Their special contribution was to send Tom and me to Lourdes in early 2001 on the 'Jumbulance,' a specially converted bus, which enabled the sick to travel. We had been to Lourdes some years before, escorting the sick daughter of a friend. Now, we were to learn an important lesson, as it was our turn to accept the help of others.

On board the Jumbulance were sixteen reclining seats for the less incapacitated pilgrims and helpers, and six bunk beds for the more seriously ill passengers. The vehicle was manned solely by volunteers, including a driver, pilgrimage leader, doctor, and two nurses. In addition, each pilgrim was accompanied by their own carer. All the sick were referred to as VIPs and were treated as such for the entire trip. For most of them, travelling by Jumbulance not only made the trip possible, but in many cases, fulfilled a lifelong dream.

Facilities on board were excellent, including a toilet and kitchen, where drinks and snacks could be prepared during the long, seventeen-hour journey.

The Leader, John Cardwell, a retired policeman and veteran of many pilgrimages, who had been honoured by the Police Force for a courageous saving of a drowning man, was also the recipient of a Papal Award for his long service to the Jumbulance.

Although Tom could not speak, the two men struck up an instant bond and on the very first day in Lourdes, John took over from me in pushing Tom's wheelchair and insisted on doing so for the entire pilgrimage. By the time the pilgrimage was over, we felt as if we had known John all our lives. I remember him once saying, sadly, "I wish I had known Tom before his stroke. I know we could have been great friends." It was obvious the feeling in Tom was mutual, but we finally had to part at the end of the pilgrimage.

In June 2001, we were able to rekindle the acquaintance with John, when he and his wife attended our fiftieth wedding anniversary. It was then that John popped the question, "Are you coming again on the next pilgrimage?"

It was not surprising, I suppose, when Tom indicated he would very much like to go, but I needed to give it some thought, as the pilgrimage was very taxing on the carer. A decision did not have to be made immediately, so it went on the back burner in my mind. Perhaps a family member could fill my place to give me some respite? A few months later, and with this dilemma still unresolved, the Lord's plan began to unfold.

One Sunday morning, as I was taking Tom's wheelchair out of our mobility vehicle to attend Mass, a man from our parish called out to me. He was just finishing smoking a cigarette before going into church when he noticed us. It was Roger, and he and his wife Sarah had been a great support when Tom was still in hospital, visiting him many times.

What Roger said next blew my mind. "Last night, I couldn't sleep. A thought was going over and over in my mind – *Go to Lourdes and take Tom with you.*"

I was utterly flabbergasted by this, because Roger knew nothing about Tom wanting to return to Lourdes and I certainly had not so much as hinted at it.

After thanking him most graciously, I declined his kind offer, saying that to look after Tom for ten days was almost too much for me and I was by then a seasoned carer. No, it was an extremely kind offer, but I could not hear of it. We walked pensively into Mass and sat in our usual places.

After Mass, Roger approached me again saying he had had time to think and pray about it, but still he felt called to take Tom to Lourdes. So it was that Tom made another trip.

It so happened that Roger had met John Cardwell at our fiftieth anniversary, so when John heard Roger was accompanying Tom, he arranged for the three men to share a room so that he and Roger could attend to Tom's needs.

When Tom returned, it was obvious he had had a wonderful time, and several people from the group sent me photographs of Roger (a former high-ranking officer in the Army) encouraging Tom to 'march' on the patio, despite the fact Tom could barely walk. It must have been marvellous for Tom to have male company after being surrounded by a world of female carers.

Thereafter, the three men were referred to as Big Roger, Big John, and Big Tom, for they were all well over six feet tall. Incredible as it may seem, Tom actually outlived the two men by several years.

Thank God for these two men. They probably never realised what a blessing they were in our time of need.

Once again, through Roger's obedience to God's voice, we had experienced God's providence. The following verses come to mind:

'And my God will meet all your needs...'
(Philippians 4:19)

'Take delight in the Lord and
He will give you the desires of your heart'
(Psalm 37:4)

ACTIONS SPEAK LOUDER
THAN WORDS
c.2006

Often people used to ask me if Tom's illness affected his faith. The reply to this question was not difficult to demonstrate if you were ever at Sunday Mass when we were there, when The Creed, several statements expressing the Catholic faith, was recited.

Tom would be following the Mass and, anticipating the recitation of the Creed, would begin to indicate to me that he was shortly going to need my assistance to stand with the rest of the congregation for this solemn moment. At this point, Tom would struggle to his feet, with my help, proudly stretching himself upright to the full measure of his six feet, two inches stature.

You could not find a more apt way for him to confirm his beliefs than in this gesture, given that The Creed starts with the words `I BELIEVE.'

Having said that, another anecdote springs to mind where Tom also shows quite clearly the importance of his faith.

As already mentioned, since Tom had his stroke, he had been unable to speak, save for a very unreliable, "yes" or "no," unreliable because he could not select the one he actually wanted, making communication extremely difficult at times.

I had become used to playing a game similar to *Twenty Questions*, a TV game played by a panel of players who were allowed to ask only direct questions, which may or may not lead to a player correctly guessing the object, word or phrase, within a given number of questions. In this case, twenty questions. The only difference between the panel game and our life, was that the questions could be endless, because Tom rarely gave up, even after many attempts to convey his need. I was often totally exhausted in the attempt. On one such occasion, I had worked out that Tom wanted to see someone in Yateley, rather urgently. Having worked my way through most of the names of friends listed in our address book, I was completely at a loss. I had also spent many hours driving around Yateley, hoping Tom would recognise where he had in mind. On more than one occasion, I stopped outside a house to which he had pointed and made enquiries of the householder if he or she knew Tom. I did this because Tom was well known by many people whom he had taken to hospital appointments. His popularity became obvious to me on several occasions when pushing him around in his wheelchair. Complete strangers would approach us and greet him. They were the clientele of Yateley Neighbourcare, (where Tom had previously been a volunteer) so I although I did not know them, they knew Tom.

After many futile attempts to allay Tom's and my own frustrations, he seemed to have forgotten about it for the moment and I eventually gave up the quest.

Then, one day, Joan the carer came to look after Tom for a few hours to give me a little respite. In order to spare Joan the frustration of trying to work out what Tom wanted, I suddenly had a flash of inspiration and asked her if she would push Tom in his wheelchair to wherever he directed. We had learned from experience that Tom's orientation was quite intact, and we jokingly used to say, "Follow that finger" as Tom gave directions. Usually this paid off but it had also been known to lead to a frustrating dead end. One never knew how it would go. Still, should this prove the case this time, at least they would have enjoyed a breath of fresh air. So, off they went on their great adventure.

When two hours had passed and they still had not returned, I began to wonder if Joan had followed the finger and forgotten to turn back! Eventually, the wanderers did return and were obviously excited to tell me of their adventure.

Joan did faithfully 'follow the finger' and surprisingly this led her to our church, St Swithun's and to Father Dominic. Once inside the church, Tom immediately led Joan to the confessional. He wanted to go to confession! So, this was what had been on his mind for the past two weeks! I never would have guessed that, even given two hundred questions.

As it so happened, when Joan knocked on the office door, she was pleasantly surprised to see the parish secretary was a familiar face from their days as young mothers. When Joan explained the reason for this unexpected call, Carole immediately read Tom's intention and went to find Father

Dominic. Without a moment's hesitation, he welcomed Tom and Joan, directing Joan to take Tom into church, where he would meet them near the Confessional, whilst he went to collect his Stole, the symbol of his priestly office. Whilst Tom was alone with Father Dominic, Joan was to ask Carole, at Father Dominic's request, to put the kettle on for coffee and cake later.

You might ask, how could Father Dominic 'hear' the confession of a man without speech? He merely listened to the intention of Tom's heart, after Joan explained how persistent Tom had been in portraying his needs. It was obvious that words were not necessary, for, as they say, "Actions speak louder than words." Tom came home looking like "the cat that got the cream."

RECOGNITION
September 2008

I thought Tom's experience with his flying application in the RAF was perhaps unique, but many years later, after Tom had suffered his stroke, I took him on a cruise to the Mediterranean. On occasion passengers were allowed to go up to the bridge with the captain. We had somehow managed this, despite being encumbered somewhat by his wheelchair. There were maps everywhere and these caught Tom's immediate attention, as navigation had been part of his duties as a Flight Engineer, besides which, he had taught navigation to our local Air Cadets in Yateley.

Possibly intrigued by Tom's obvious interest, the captain came over to us. I explained Tom's lack of speech, so spoke for him. Before long I was telling him of Tom's desire to become a pilot and his failed application due to his northern accent. The captain's response was immediate. His application to become a captain in the Royal Navy had also been turned down, for the very same reason! Consequently, he had pursued a career in the Merchant Navy, whose sights were perhaps less blinkered.

Speaking for Tom, as I had become accustomed to doing,

made me realise on occasions like this just how much our lives had become entwined. Tom was *living through me* just as I was living in the present through our shared memories and history.

Pauline and Tom

An immediate rapport developed between the captain and Tom, and he spent quite some time pointing to various navigational maps dotted around the walls, talking technically to Tom in a way that indicated that he recognised in Tom the professional mind he still had, despite his lack of speech. It was heart-warming to see this played out between the two men and to see Tom literally coming alive by simply being recognised for the person he truly was. It was worth any amount of sacrifice on my part.

Maybe this was the best explanation for my resistance to Tom being placed in a care home. He would have withered inside without the mouthpiece I had become and my heart would have broken completely to watch this happen.

Welling up in my heart were the sentiments written on a wall plaque given to me by Tom many years earlier which I could now apply equally to him.

> *"I love you, not only for what you are,*
> *But for what I am when I am with you"*

IT IS FINISHED

It was just another day when a scream of panic alerted me from the next room, where the new carer was attempting to feed Tom. The scream could be heard all over the house. Rushing immediately towards the sound, I found Tom choking and struggling to breathe.

Immediately after dealing with the present situation, I called the doctor for further advice. He promised to come as soon as possible. In the meantime, I had composed myself with the knowledge that we had faced this ordeal once before and survived it.

For some time, the doctor had been warning that feeding Tom by mouth was becoming increasingly dangerous and, indeed, might be becoming too hazardous. If the food had entered the lungs, which was feared, he might develop pneumonia, with a catastrophic outcome. The thought of his having to be fed by a feeding tube into the stomach filled me with great sadness for Tom. The stroke had already deprived him of so much in life, and the thought of having to be fed by a feeding tube for the rest of his life would deny him the pleasure of eating, one of the few remaining pleasures left to him.

The doctor's prognosis when he arrived was that Tom's best chance of survival was to have him admitted to hospital immediately. The initial concern was to discover whether the food had entered his lungs. Unfortunately, this was the case and the next several days were spent x-raying him and monitoring the onset and development of pneumonia, as predicted.

Just when Tom was showing some signs of improvement, he suddenly developed a strange rapid breathing pattern, interspersed with alternate lapses into unconsciousness. Whenever he did become conscious, it was only momentarily, during which time he would stare at me with fear, or urgency in his eyes, each time attempting to communicate something of great importance. Meanwhile, the doctors were baffled and could give no accurate diagnosis. By means of brain scans we learned, eventually, that the lapses into unconsciousness were due to seizures occurring.

Visit by Father Dominic
At this point, I decided to invite our parish priest, Father Dominic, to minister the Sacrament of the Sick. Father Dominic agreed to come as soon as possible, so on the day proposed, I spent the whole day at the hospital awaiting his visit. My friend Donna came after work to visit, around 5.30pm and still Father Dominic had not arrived. Meanwhile, I was just telling her that Tom had hardly been conscious at all that day and probably would not be able to appreciate the visit even if and when Father Dominic did come.

Minutes later, Father Dominic arrived on the ward, facing in my direction. Donna on the other side of the bed did not see him approach but monitored what followed with growing amazement. Meanwhile, Tom was still unconscious, as he had been for most of the day.

Then the miracle* happened. When Father Dominic was about three feet away from the bedside, Tom suddenly sprang into full consciousness, as if recognising his mere presence. Donna attests to this 'miracle' to this day.

Opening his eyes, Tom saw Father Dominic, smiled, and held out his hand in welcome, offering him his special handshake! This is an African sign of peace, which we had experienced on a trip to Nairobi some years before, and which Tom had sometimes adopted as his own means of welcome since losing the power of speech. It was so appropriate, too, to use it now with Father Dominic, who was himself African, and could fully appreciate the sentiments expressed through it.

Closing the curtains around the bed space to afford privacy, Father Dominic knew exactly what Tom wanted - and proceeded to go through a confessional process. Tom needed only to respond with a Yes or a No, indicated by a nod of the head, to a series of questions, after which Father Dominic blessed him, anointing him with holy oil, then spent the remainder of the time chatting and offering comforting and encouraging remarks.

Father Dominic could only stay for a short time because he had just collected another priest from the airport who would be staying for a few days, but he promised to return again soon. As far as we knew at that time, Tom's death was not imminent.

Father Dominic had barely left the ward when Tom lapsed back into a state of unconsciousness, as he had been for most of the day. The miracle was that little window of consciousness when Father Dominic visited, allowing Tom to make what would be his final confession and anointing. Now Tom was finally at peace within himself and with God.

Visit by Brian and Judy – and another miracle
A decision had to be made soon regarding Tom's feeding method and the decision was no longer one option versus another. The only way Tom could receive nourishment safely would be by a tube into the stomach. Within the next few days, he was measured up for the operation and was expected to return home once the operation was complete and I had been taught how to monitor safely the feeding process.

Taking care of Tom ever since the stroke had been a huge learning curve, but this stage promised to be the greatest challenge so far. Who could I turn to for advice once we were alone at home? Then I remembered Brian and Judy were in the same predicament. Brian had Parkinson's Disease and had been managing with a feeding tube for a few years now. The thought reassured me. I could ask them for advice.

Unfortunately, we had lost contact in recent years due to our busy caring roles and they had also moved house and I did not have their forwarding address. Fortunately, they knew friends of ours from the parish, but on making enquiries, I learned that they were presently away on holiday, so I was unable to follow up on this lead.

It was at this stage that we were blessed with another miracle. Tom had still not had the procedure carried out, when one day as I was walking down the hospital corridor, I heard my name being called from behind. Turning around, I was astonished to see it was none other than Brian and Judy, just about to leave the hospital!

After a momentary gasp of surprise and mutual recognition, I blurted out that for days I had been trying to get in touch with them. Judy's response was immediate, "Well, you know prayer works!"

Once the surprise of this 'chance' meeting had subsided and the reason for my being there explained, they immediately decided to return to Tom's ward to pray for him, which was what Tom had been trying to communicate to me for weeks. I had worked my way through our address book until I came across their names, when he had given a vigorous nod of the head. They had called several times in the past and prayed with Tom, besides which, when Brian could still speak, the two men could 'talk' aeroplanes, as Brian had been a Pilot and Tom a Flight Engineer in their former lives. Both of our prayers would be answered that day. Tom wanted their prayerful support, and I needed their support and possible practical advice in the future.

On the day I called, You answered me;
You increased my strength of soul.
(NRSV Psalms 138:3)

Brian and Judy went ahead of me because they were in a hurry to keep another appointment, so by the time I reached the ward, they had already prayed with Tom. I could tell this by the expression on his face! Brian and Judy had gone, but the pure joy on Tom's face told me that their mission had been accomplished. When I had left Tom, he had been unconscious for hours but now he was once again fully conscious and grinning from ear to ear! Through that chance meeting with Brian and Judy, we had worked out what Tom has been requesting of me for weeks. What is more, he had been granted another window of consciousness, to savour those precious moments of prayer, for soon he would lapse into unconsciousness again and would die less than twenty-four hours later, a peaceful and holy death.

Although his death was a shock, sudden and unexpected, I began to realise that God's timing is perfect, and all of my prayer requests had been answered.

The Eve of the Funeral – The Chaplet of Divine Mercy
It had rained almost incessantly the whole week of the funeral and I had been anxiously watching the weather forecast because, after the funeral Mass, there was to be a short service at the graveside.

I did not have a decent raincoat to wear in case of inclement weather, so decided to pop along to M&S to see if there was anything suitable. Before going however, I called Rose, the carer and Donna, my friend, to say with me *The Chaplet of Divine Mercy* on Tom's behalf.

The 'Chaplet' had become Tom's favourite prayer form because he was able to participate, in part. Although he could not speak words, we had become aware that he could hum a tune. The first time we experienced this was when I had a group of friends round for a social evening. Each of us had agreed to perform a song, give a recitation, perform a party trick, play an instrument, whatever each could contribute. We even had one who was a professional dancer who tap danced her way up and down the tiled floor of the kitchen, which was adjacent to the dining room. I remember I recited the famous monologue, *Albert and the Lion*, made famous by Stanley Holloway. After the laughter had subsided, we became aware of a thin, weak voice humming, recognisably, the tune to *Danny Boy*. It was Tom's first communication beyond a nod of the head and that special handshake.

In latter times, when praying with Tom in the evening, he was able to hum along to the tune when I played the recording of *The Chaplet of Divine Mercy*. Being able to participate, even in this limited way, gave him great peace and satisfaction. Donna and Rose both knew that we prayed/sung the Chaplet most evenings, so in Tom's memory, we prayed it once more.

While the Chaplet was being sung, I reflected on the many graces we had been granted during our marriage, thanking God for all His favours.

Finally, as a silence settled on us, I distinctly heard in my spirit, "It is finished," echoing the last words of Jesus (*"It is Finished." NIV John 19:30*). This is often interpreted as meaning, "It is accomplished or completed."

By these words, I felt the Lord was saying that everything Tom had been sent to do on this earth had been accomplished, was completed. With this thought, I could no longer grieve but found great consolation.

It was later pointed out to me that perhaps these words were addressed to, and for, me, also. Just as the lady in the Stroke Club had cared for her husband for twelve years, so, too, had I. God had given me the strength, day by day. All my prayers for Tom's care had come to fruition. I had outlived him; I had coped with his needs to the end, including managing to care for him at home, and now he did not have to go through the additional ordeal of being fed through a feeding tube.

Blessings at the Funeral

The funeral Mass went beautifully and with precision, thanks to all the family. The beautiful Order of Service had been prepared by our daughter-in-law, Kay; young grandson, Joe, with grandson Tom's assistance, distributing them as people arrived.

The coffin was borne by our sons, (Stephen and Peter), grandsons, (Matthew and Tom), Tom's brother (Leo) and son-in-law (Tony). During the service, granddaughters Sophie and Sarah read the Scripture passages; Stephen read the Prayers of Thanksgiving, and Sarah and her school friend sang *Panis Angelicus* - one of Tom's favourite hymns.

In fact, they sang it twice because of its brevity, and the obvious enthusiasm with which it was received. Finally, our daughter, Anne, gave a wonderful eulogy in honour of her father. It is not usual to applaud in church, because the focus is on God not ourselves, but someone led the applause and soon the whole church was clapping, in recognition of Tom and the wonderful man he was known to be.

And could anyone forget that final hymn, the African American Spiritual *Going Home* - chosen by Tom twenty-two years previously, with the accompanying note, "Please do not hear this as a sentimental tear-jerker, but as a statement of my faith in the resurrection of all who believe in Jesus."

Because I led the funeral procession out of the church, I only heard the first verse, but the choirmaster told me later that the choir could hardly sing it, they were so choked with emotion.

And I heard there were many tears shed by the congregation - tears not so much of sadness, but of loving respect for a man who had suffered horrendous isolation and frustration during his long years without speech, yet who still had a fun-loving sense of humour and an evangelising spirit, as a final anecdote portrays.

Blackbushe Farewell

At the graveside, Father Dominic paid another little tribute to Tom, just as a small plane from nearby Blackbushe Airport passed overhead, commenting "how appropriate for Tom" as he looked upwards. It was almost like a flypast in recognition, I thought, after which Father Dominic burst into singing my favourite hymn, *How Great Thou Art*.

Ongoing Graces

Two days later was a Sunday and I went to Mass, sitting in my usual place, experiencing for the first time Mass without Tom at my side.

Quietly, someone called Maureen slipped into the pew next to me. We had come to know her during the seven months when Tom was in Fleet hospital. Maureen was an assistant to the Physio there and got to know us during Tom's physio sessions, which I usually attended.

What was Maureen doing here, I thought, knowing that she attended the Anglican Church. Before I could ask the question, she blurted out that after attending Tom's funeral, she just had to attend a Sunday Catholic Mass, because she had been so impressed with our funeral rite. I did not even know she had attended the funeral because of the large numbers there!

She stayed beside me for the remainder of the Mass and the next I heard was that she was thinking of becoming a Catholic! Even more surprising, sometime later I received a call from Father Dominic asking me to prepare Maureen to be received into the Church! The Lord had already prepared me for this very role when I had studied Pastoral Theology, a few years earlier, so I had the privilege of catechising and preparing her to join the Catholic Church. But I think Tom had been the real evangelist and teacher. It was his courageous example in dealing with his disabilities, and his sense of fun, which had attracted her to the source of his strength, his Catholic faith.

"Evangelise at all times – if necessary, with words."
(Anon but often attributed to St Francis)

*Miracle – an extraordinary event taken as a sign of the power of God

WITH US TILL THE END

CALLED BY NAME

No matter how far nor how long we may have strayed from God, there comes a time in our lives, I believe, when we finally become aware of that 'still small voice' of God, calling us back to Him. Such a time came in Donna's life, through a particular set of circumstances, but before proceeding with her story, I want to pause to consider, 'What's in a name'?

There was a time when names were chosen by parents not so much for how they sounded but for what they meant. This has an ancient tradition, going back to Biblical times, when individuals were called in memory of past heroes, great men or women, or perhaps a well-loved member of the family, but usually they denoted a particular quality or virtue, which it was hoped would define their character or calling. An obvious example from the Old Testament was Abram, later named Abraham by God, (Abraham meaning Father of many nations), because of the promise by God to make his descendants "as many as the grains of sand on the seashore." Despite this being most unlikely, since Abraham was one hundred-years-old at the time and his wife was ninety, indeed a child was born to them, by God's grace, and so Abraham's seed was passed on to countless numbers over the centuries.

Moving into the New Testament, the various titles given to Jesus – 'Emmanuel' meaning 'God with us' and 'Jesus' meaning 'He who saves' or 'Saviour' defined exactly who Jesus was and why He came. Later, Jesus was to change the name of Simon to Peter, meaning 'Rock', to define the purpose of the change of name when he said that Peter (Rock) was to be the foundation on which His church was to be built.

With that little detour, I now wish to talk about Donna (meaning God's Gift). I do not know if her parents were aware of its meaning when they so named her, but she certainly has been God's gift to me in so many ways since I first became acquainted with her.

It was in January 2010 when we first met. At that time, we had a visiting priest from Spain, dear Father Seve. He was in the parish for the second or third time, standing in for our priest who had gone on leave for his usual post-Christmas holiday.

Tom's stroke had occurred since Father Seve's last visit and he was deeply saddened to see what had happened to him, so made a point of coming to see Tom every day. Despite Father Seve's protestations to walk to our house, I decided to pick him up after morning Mass.

Father Seve is one of those priests who is happiest among the people and so he had invited the few weekday Mass attendees into the presbytery kitchen for a warm drink. It was there that I met Donna. I quickly glanced around the room; the other faces were all known to me, but I had never met her before, so I introduced myself. I was surprised when she said that she knew who I was, or at least she knew who had put the item in the parish newsletter advertising an Advent course. She went on to explain that she had been interested but did not feel confident enough to get in touch.

A little further into our conversation, Donna said that she had stopped attending Church when she was 15 but had recently returned after 35 years absence! I was flabbergasted and wanted to know what had prompted her return. A truly amazing story emerged. The church choir had organised a concert on the eve of Palm Sunday, which caught Donna's interest. During the concert, she experienced something very strange. Over and above the singing, she could hear her name being called, over and over again, "Donna, Donna."

At some point in the evening, mention was made of it being Palm Sunday the next day. This evoked long-forgotten memories of times in her childhood when she had attended Palm Sunday Mass, and she recalled the processions and the singing of "Alleluias," just as the people of Jerusalem had done on that first Palm Sunday. The memory prompted her decision to attend Mass the following day, after which she started to attend each Sunday. At some stage, she introduced herself to the then resident priest, Father Dominic, and was received back into the Church. She had, however, been attending about a year but nobody, not a single person, had welcomed her or even spoken to her, and she was on the verge of giving up on Church again when we met.

Taking up on the interest she had shown regarding the

Advent group, I invited her to the concluding session of the Advent course that evening.

During the meeting, as usual we studied and unpacked the meanings of the Scriptures for the following Sunday. The particular Gospel was from John's gospel, where he declares, "Behold the Lamb of God" - pointing to Jesus. Immediately, Donna's attention was riveted by these words. Since coming back to Church, she explained, she had heard these words repeated at Mass week by week but did not understand what they meant. Now, her eyes had been opened and it was obvious that she was ready for more. I told her, in front of the group, that although the sessions had now officially come to an end, I was still prepared to carry on with her, and was thrilled when the group agreed to keep on meeting for Donna's sake. Although it has not always been the same group, a small nucleus continued, and Donna met with us weekly for over seven years. We supported her through the RCIA process (Rite of Christian Initiation of Adults), giving her a good grounding in the Catholic Faith. She is now strong in her faith and has taken on various ministries in the Church, most notably becoming a regular Reader at Mass.

Donna - 'God's Gift' to Me in Time of Illness

From late December 2011 to February 2012, I suffered from a sudden onset of heart failure, from which I was not expected to survive. However, the Lord had other plans for my life, and I came through, though it took two months to drain the enormous amount of fluid that had collected in my legs and abdomen. During my time in hospital, Donna was a frequent visitor, coming straight from work sometimes. But most times she would be one of my later visitors. In fact, she usually waited for the others to leave, when she would then turn into nursing mode (she is a nurse) and would cream my legs and feet, which were extremely dry from the medications, drainage procedure and restricted fluid intake. She will never fully appreciate how grateful I was for her loving attention to me.

Donna - 'God's Gift' to Me at the Time of Tom's Death

Donna was present at two very significant moments in the last weeks of Tom's life, including being present at his death. I have written elsewhere about this, so I shall not repeat it here. I very often used to say that Donna has been more like a daughter to me than a friend. She is very close in age to my children, and it so happened that when Tom died, my daughter, Anne, was away on a special holiday to celebrate her twenty-fifth wedding anniversary. Had she been in England, it would have been Anne who would have been with me, but God provided support for me, through Donna. I have always thought of her as 'God's Gift' and she has certainly lived up to that name in my life.

Donna has been a wonderful daughter to her parents and has certainly been 'God's Gift' to them in more ways than one. In her adult life, she trained as a Psychiatric nurse, working for fourteen years with drug and alcohol abuse victims where, I am sure, she has most definitely been 'God's Gift' to so many, by assisting victims to break free of their dependencies. Truly, her naming was most apt!

"...I have called you by your name, you are mine"
(Berean Standard Bible Isaiah 43:1)

ROMANS 8:28
May 2015

Don't presume anything! This was one of two things I was to learn that day. The first was the truth of this saying when I checked in at the reception of my local hospital. Right time, wrong hospital!

Since last attending Outpatients, a new satellite hospital had been opened to lessen the strain on the main hospital. Having always been used to attending the main hospital, I had presumed my appointment was at that one. Now here I was, early for my appointment there, but not early enough to drive across town to the other hospital! Fortunately, the consultant had another clinic in the early afternoon, so I was booked into that one instead.

This mistake would call for a change of my plans for the rest of the morning but would set into motion God's plan for me that day! I had thought to go for coffee with my friend, Anne Thal after my appointment. Now I would have to call to change our plans.

Immediately Anne heard of my predicament she suggested we could have lunch together instead, after which I could return to the original hospital, where I had been re-booked into the afternoon clinic.

When I arrived at Anne's, she was wearing a T-shirt with words and numbers printed on it, spelling out the message ROMANS 8.28. Even on Anne's ample bosom, she had not attempted to spell out what the Scripture verse said! It was not a verse I was familiar with, so I let her explain. The quotation is:

"All things work together for good for those who love God, who are called according to His purpose."
(NSRV Romans: 8:28)

On my return to the hospital in the afternoon, I had time to spare, so decided to get a coffee and wait in the restaurant. I happened to be using my mobility scooter that day, so needed assistance to carry my coffee over to a table. Unfortunately, no tables were free, but a lady nearest to me saw the predicament and offered to share the table with her and another lady.

Having settled in the space offered, I introduced myself to the ladies and tried to become as inconspicuous as possible, so they could resume their conversation. Instead, they immediately included me in their chat. They were not friends exactly, one was there on an appointment, the other was a volunteer driver. This offered an opening to say that my husband had been a volunteer driver before he died.

I was attending hospital that day for a referral to the ENT specialist about a worrisome throat condition. The mere thought of having my throat examined filled me with dread because I have a very sensitive gag reflex. The fear must have been etched in my face as I said the words, so when one of the ladies leaned in towards me, apparently to utter some reassuring words, I was astonished to hear, *"Remember, Romans 8:28: 'All things work togetherfor good for those who love God..."*

That day was the first time I had heard these words, and now they were being voiced for a second time! Immediately, the peace of God came over me, and I knew for certain this was His reassurance to me. I no longer feared the examination.

The conversation moved on and I went on to tell them an amusing story set in this very restaurant. The place where I used to work, Marconi Space and Defence Systems, is close by the hospital. One day at work, the emergency fire alarm sounded as a fire drill and all two thousand workers filed into the grounds. Whilst waiting there, one of the men from the Christian Fellowship spotted me and came over so we could wait together.

After ten minutes or so had passed, Alan suggested we go over to the hospital restaurant for a coffee instead of waiting outside in the cold. This sounded like a good idea, so off we went. We became so engrossed in conversation, however, that we quite forgot the time and more than an hour had slipped by without our noticing. When we hurriedly returned to the site, we discovered that everyone had been allowed back in just ten minutes after we left! Fortunately, I had my own office so was not missed.

At the mention of Marconi, the volunteer lady mentioned that her husband used to work there and perhaps I knew him. This was hardly likely since it was more than thirty years since I had worked there. Nevertheless, she mentioned her husband by name. I thought, for less than a minute, then uttered in recognition, "Tall, military bearing, with a moustache." 'You've got him in one!" she replied. The reason I knew him was because he was a Project Manager who reported to my boss!

I had often wondered if my boss was still alive. We had such a good working relationship. In his spare time, he was a member of the Samaritans, in fact, he trained them. It was he who first suggested that I should consider becoming a counsellor. It was in the recalling of these happy memories that prompted me to ask if my former boss were still alive. "Yes, they meet up once a month," she responded.

It was nearing time for my appointment, but I could not let this opportunity go by without sending a message to my former boss. Writing on the only paper available, a paper napkin, I wrote a hurried message, thanking him for the happy working relationship we had once enjoyed.

Soon, it would be time for me to make my way towards the clinic. Where I had once dreaded it, now I was calm, reassured by the amazing 'coincidences' I had experienced that day. The Lord had shown clearly that He is with us at every moment. He knew of the mistaken appointment and had allowed it. Without my apparent mistake, I would not have met that lady, would not have heard the Scripture repeated for a second time and the impact it had upon me.

With these thoughts in mind, I moved to my appointment and am pleased to say that the examination was carried out through the nose, so I had no gag reflex and nothing sinister was found!

Had I gone through this whole exercise just to bring this set of circumstances into play? The Scripture that day was certainly fulfilled, and it has since become a favourite quotation of mine.

It would be lovely to say that my message found its way to my boss and we re-connected, but I never heard anything further. I can only presume that the lady lost the napkin, because I am sure my boss would have called me otherwise. On the other hand, how did I start this reflection - Never presume!

Whatever the truth of the matter is, *"ALL THINGS WORK TOGETHER FOR GOOD FOR THOSE WHO LOVE GOD..."*

ONE MAN'S TRASH
August 2016

During the years when the prayer group met, I had amassed a considerable number of spiritual books, some were the spiritual classics, others were popular reads of more recent times. These formed our lending library, made up of my own books and others donated by the group as they finished reading them.

It was now many years since the group had disbanded and I needed to make a decision about the books, for I was quickly running out of space on which to display them. In their time they had been a precious resource, but now the prayer group no longer existed, logic dictated I dispose of them, but how? It was hard to just throw them out.

As so often happens with difficult decisions, I procrastinated for quite some time before making the inevitable decision to dispose of them, or at least some of them. To relegate them to the rubbish tip seemed almost sacrilegious, so I came up with another solution. The local charity shop had a bookshelf for donated books, so I lodged them there, hopeful that somebody might give them a second life.

It was now a Saturday evening, and I was just settling

down to watch TV when the telephone rang. A man's voice at the other end was querying whether he was speaking with Pauline Doyle. Introducing himself by name did not enlighten me, as far as I knew he was a stranger. But he continued, with obvious enthusiasm in his voice. "You don't know me, but I found your name and telephone number in the front cover of a book I have just read and I am just ringing to thank you and to tell you that it has changed my life!"

The rest of the conversation is a blur. I cannot even remember the title of the book. All I do remember is the tingle of excitement this news brought, as I recalled the old adage that 'One man's trash is another man's treasure!' Or more biblically,

> *"Cast your bread upon the waters*
> *for after many days*
> *you will find it again."*
> *(Berean Standard Bible Ecclesiastes 11:1).*

BLESSINGS FROM ALICANTE
23Rd June 2017

Just as our bible study meeting was coming to a close, Margherita extended an invitation to us to attend a House Mass in her home on the Friday evening, followed by a shared supper. She often spoke of a community of monks and nuns in Alicante, which she visits for her annual retreat. She spoke especially fondly of the beloved Founder of this community of monks, Father Umberto.

In the Catholic Church, it is not so easy to set up a new Order, yet when Father Umberto met the late Saint Pope Paul II with a view to asking permission to set up his Order, apparently there was an instant rapport between the two men and amazingly, within two days, the Pope gave his blessing for the Order to be founded. For over 20 years, it flourished under Father Umberto's guidance and soon lay people were also joining, hence Margherita's contact with them. Sadly, Father Umberto has since died, but his legacy lives on and the monks continue his vision. Margherita often speaks of the wisdom of his teaching.

Now, two lay members and one of the monks, a certain

Father Lazaro, were coming over to Margherita's and our bible study group was being invited. I was both delighted and intrigued to meet them.

I duly arrived with a plate of food to be shared at the supper following the Mass and took up a convenient place in the lounge where Mass was to be celebrated. Meanwhile, latecomers congregated in the garden, socialising until called inside. Because of this, I met Father Lazaro, as he was putting final touches to the altar and discussing how he planned to conduct the Mass. He had been busy translating into English some well-known hymns, so we could participate and was trying them out, accompanying himself on his guitar. We chatted for some time as he busied himself with the preparations and I felt very relaxed in his company.

Just before Mass was about to start, Margherita and he were running through the plans, when Father Lazaro announced that he wanted to give his homily in Spanish because his English was not adequate for what he had to impart. I looked at Margherita with a questioning look. How would we understand? Her reply astonished me when she said, "This is where the Holy Spirit comes in." Apparently, she is given a special charism, the ability to translate even though she has never learned the language! The Gift, remarkably, is only 'loaned' to her exclusively for the Sacred Mass. Margherita, whose native language is Italian cannot understand everyday Spanish, even simple words!

Sure enough, as the Mass progressed and we came to the homily, Margherita was given the Gift by the Holy Spirit and was able to translate, sentence by sentence. The accuracy of her translation was confirmed the next day by another Spanish speaking person from our group. This was exactly what happened at Pentecost when Peter spoke to the crowd. All could hear in their own native language! (See Acts Ch.2). How wonderful that the Holy Spirit still wants to impart His gifts, if we are open to them!

From beginning to end, the Mass was joyful and Father Lazaro's guitar playing and singing made it very special. There was a funny side to it all as well. Margherita keeps a set of vestments for visiting priests to wear when celebrating in her home. These vestments were far too long for Father Lazaro, so he had to keep hitching them up as he went round the room distributing Holy Communion. I was the last to receive from the Chalice and I also consumed the small piece of Host, which is placed in the Chalice, known as the 'Fraction.' I have never experienced this before and as I received it, it felt like 'a double portion,' an extra blessing. It was a very special moment.

After Holy Communion, Father Lazaro took out some holy oil, which, he explained, was from an ancient monastery where a miracle had occurred, in as much as a holy icon began to exude oil which was collected in a jar and subsequently has not needed to be replenished. Once again, he went around the room, (still hitching up his vestments) and blessed each of us with the holy oil, making the sign of the cross on our foreheads. As before, I was last to be ministered to and because I was unable to stand when he came to me, he went down on his knees to bless me and then gave me the most enormous hug and whispered, "Jesus loves you." I can tell you, that blessing and hug felt like Jesus Himself hugging me there. What a blessed moment.

But there was more to come, food to share and fellowship to enjoy. As Mass ended, we all transferred into the kitchen/dining room, where a long table had been laid, with seating for all sixteen of us. While people were still coming in, Father Lazaro picked up his guitar once again and started to play wonderful Spanish flamenco-style music. The Spanish couple present clapped and danced to it, much to our enjoyment. Then, we sat down to eat. I was fortunate enough to sit next to Father Lazaro and we had an interesting talk about the Holy Spirit in our lives.

After supper, Father Lazaro once again started to play and amidst the various tunes I suddenly recognised Paul McCartney's song, *Let it be*, which we all joined in, singing with gusto. But Father Lazaro had other talents. He told us so many jokes our sides were nearly splitting. All clean jokes, I might add! In fact, I remarked to myself how much funnier and life-giving are good, simple jokes instead of what passes for jokes on our media.

As the evening was closing, Father Lazaro started to play the Community's song, which they sing to the tune of *Edelweiss*, after which we all sang the song in English, bringing the evening to a pleasant close.

I was so blessed that evening, I just wanted to record it here. I did not want it to be lost in all the busyness of life. It was a very special evening and I drove home on a high, with the tune of *Edelweiss* ringing in my ears. On returning home, I was unable to sleep with sheer joy until 5 am.

Thank you, dear Holy Spirit, for your amazing Presence among us that evening. What a privilege! What a Gift!

SWAHILI BLESSING
1St October 2020

Miracles, some large, some small, occur every day; most of the time without our even being aware of them. Fortunately, occasionally, our spiritual eyes are sufficiently open to glimpse the Hand of God at work in our lives.

The above date, 1st October, is one I have held dear ever since I met my beloved late husband, Tom. This was his birthday.

The date came into significance again many years later when faced with corrective surgery for glaucoma. It was a tricky procedure, which appeared to have been successful initially, but over time, the pressure in the eye slowly began to decrease to a dangerous level, endangering my sight. The options I had were - do nothing and eventually lose the sight, or have a further operation to correct the fault, which came with its own risks, one of which was to lose my sight anyway. I chose to go for the op.

Because of the seriousness of the situation, I hoped a date for the operation would not be overly delayed due to the Covid 19 situation, which was taking precedence over other treatments. Enquiring about his waiting list (the consultant had earlier proffered that he himself wanted to carry out the operation), he simply said, "six weeks" not, "about" or "maybe" but, "six weeks," which I later calculated took us to 1st October, an auspicious date to me, for the reason already stated.

As the weeks passed leading up to the operation, church friends reminded me that I had my own dear saint (Tom) in heaven to pray for me. This thought gave me comfort and courage to face the forthcoming ordeal.

The day of the operation finally dawned and I was surprised to find that I was not at all nervous as the pre-op procedures were carried out. Once inside the operating theatre, the surgeon impressed upon the theatre staff that I needed to be made as comfortable as possible, as the surgery was expected to take around forty-five minutes and I had to remain motionless whilst he performed two delicate operations. The first operation was routine cataract surgery, which would stabilise the eye, enabling the surgeon to attend to the corrective surgery. He did, however, promise a five-minute break between the two surgeries. As it turned out, with the unexpected additional surgery it took over ninety minutes!

Having promised a five-minute break between the two surgeries, we were 'good to go' as they say. Or not quite! One of the theatre nurses in attendance seated at my knee level, said, "Would you like me to hold your hand?" I was not surprised by the question because I had read the notes in the pre-op literature, which mentioned this. I was not nervous at all, yet jokingly found myself replying, "Who would refuse a kind offer like that?" which she took to be a "Yes."

Stretching out my hand in her direction, I expected her to take my hand in hers, as in a handshake, instead of which she merely took my thumb, wiggling it vigorously, instantly reviving a memory long since forgotten, of something I had experienced when I joined Tom on a trip to Nairobi in the early 1980s. It was on that trip that I had the dubious 'privilege' of being invited by the captain to join Tom on the flight deck for the landing in Nairobi. I say 'dubious' because at that time I was very nervous of flying, but it turned out to be one of my most memorable experiences, as I watched and heard the crew as they were being 'talked down' to Nairobi, which I followed on the set of headphones I was given. As memorable as that was, it was not that particular memory I recalled in the operating theatre but one which we both experienced when we attended Mass in the Cathedral in Nairobi a few days later.

"Do you know you have just offered me the 'Sign of Peace' in Swahili?" I said, which brought a gasp from the theatre nurse. I went on to explain.

Tom and I attended Mass twice during our stay in Nairobi. The first, in English, was rather grand with classical music and a robed choir singing but leaving the congregation (mostly ex-pats) somewhat passive, I thought.

On the second occasion, Mass was in the local language, Swahili. What a cultural difference! The people were so much more alive and spontaneous in their worship, dancing down the aisle as they carried the offerings for Holy

Communion. But it was at the 'Sign of Peace' that I experienced that special wiggling of the thumb from the old lady in front of us who had turned around to extend the gesture.

Making enquiries later, I learned that this gesture does not merely equate to "Peace be with you" as we say in English, as we shake hands. In Swahili, it is much richer than 'Peace', which can be quite weak in English and does not catch the deeper meaning conveyed in this sign, which means something like, "I wish you an inner sense of completeness and wholeness," rather like "Shalom" in Hebrew. This was the memory which the thumb wiggling had evoked. How appropriate I thought, on Tom's special day, recalling that first shared experience. It was as if Tom himself were present once again, supporting me.

It was then the nurse's turn to speak. Having so far responded merely with a gasp, she went on to say that her family originated from Kenya, and in fact her father was actually born in Nairobi but she was born here (and presumably was not necessarily aware of this local custom). Nevertheless, she had given me their traditional sign.

What an amazing set of 'coincidences' came together in that simple exchange: Firstly, the date, Tom's birthday; the memory shared with Tom in Nairobi; a theatre nurse offering me the local sign; her family connections with Kenya and especially Nairobi, her father's place of birth. Not least of these 'coincidences' is the fact that out of all the nurses in the hospital who might have been on duty that day, it would have only taken for her to be on duty another day or even another shift on that day for this set of circumstances to fail to synchronise.

Before the surgery, I had prayed for God to guide the hand of the surgeon, which was definitely needed for the unexpected surgery he was later to perform when a hole in the white of my eye was discovered! With incredible skill, he resolved the problem by making a patch by splicing a section from a layer of my own eye. On my follow up visit, his colleagues remarked on this stellar piece of surgery.

A final thought linking this episode with Tom. When he lost his speech following his stroke, he sometimes used the 'Swahili Blessing' to welcome friends who visited.

It would seem the Swahili Blessing continues.

JOURNEY'S END

Over the past forty years, since I first became aware of promptings from the Holy Spirit, He has guided me faithfully to many different lands. It seems appropriate, somehow, as I bring these precious memoirs to a close, that my recent and possibly last journey should have taken me to the northern tip of Spain, known historically as 'the ends of the earth'.

It came about when my attention was drawn to a cruise whose final outward destination was La Coruña, a name which sparked in my memory the famous poem, *The burial of Sir John Moore at the battle of Coruña* by Charles Wolfe, which I had learned by heart at school.

Even more significant than this memory was the realisation that this was the nearest port for modern day pilgrims who prefer, or who are unable to manage the full five hundred mile pilgrimage on foot, as thousands have walked over the centuries.

Journey's end for pilgrims is the famous city of Santiago de Compostela, with its magnificent cathedral, built in the ninth century, where the bones of the Apostle James, Patron Saint of Spain, are said to rest.

Left: Pauline and Anne on cruise to Spain 2022. Right: Pauline arriving on scooter at the Cathedral of Santiago de Compostela

Challenged by the relative proximity of Santiago de Compostela to La Coruña, my daughter Anne, with whom I would be travelling, arranged for us to be met at the port side by a taxi which could accommodate my mobility scooter, for exploring the cathedral environs later. Unfortunately, we underestimated the length of time needed to accommodate a meal break and comfort stops en route! One look at the long snake-like queue to enter the cathedral also indicated that it would not be possible to see inside the building before we needed to make our return journey back to the ship.

I have learned from experience that often when my plans are thwarted, God is usually engineering something even more surprising, which would prove to be the case in this instance.

Unbeknown to me at that time, my grandson Tom, who had been working on his PhD thesis on the Spanish Civil War, had been contemplating walking this sacred route known as the 'Camino' (The Way) as a means of taking a complete break from intense study and seeking the way forward for the rest of his career.

Tom unexpectedly coming across the signpost to the Camino de Santiago

While he was still mulling things over, he visited me and told me of his plans, mentioning for the first time that he felt this "was something I have to do - a kind of 'call.'" When I heard that, a tingle of excitement grew inside of me as I remembered the many promptings I had received, urging me to travel to certain places in the world. I felt privileged that he had confided this to me. Offering the wisest advice I could, that if it were a call from God, He would somehow confirm it, we left the discussion there.

The next day, or it may have been a couple of days later, an exciting email from Tom dropped into my mailbox complete with 'the sign' he had been waiting for.

Tom had taken a walk with his fiancée, Holley, whilst visiting Winchester (they both live in Southampton) when they came across a sign on a lamp post which captured his attention immediately. Beneath a straight-ahead sign was a shell symbol, the familiar sign which guides those who follow the 'Camino' route.' In Spanish were words to the effect 'English way to Santiago'. Holley's comment on eyeing the sign, with its implication for Tom, said, "Not just a metaphorical sign but a real sign! Like grandmother, like grandson." That was it! This was the obvious confirmation that Tom had been hoping for and with that, he began to prepare for his trip.

The total length of the pilgrimage is five hundred miles. Few complete the trek in one attempt, but the number of completed stages are stamped and certified. When all stages have been completed, a certificate verifying the achievement is presented to the successful pilgrim.

Eventually the day dawned when, with rucksack packed as economically as possible weight wise and with staff in hand, he set off from the French Basque region of the Pyrenees, treading the well-worn path and following the distinctive shell symbol marking the pilgrim route.

Despite painful knees negotiating a region known locally as 'the knee breaker', he continued doggedly after resting for a day and purchasing a pair of knee supports. After a while he began to be troubled with blisters on his feet, forcing him to rest for a couple of days. Despite these setbacks, he completed the entire five hundred miles in just thirty-one days and has the certificate to prove it.

The day after arriving in Santiago there was a special Pilgrims' Mass, which he attended, and by means of photographs taken from inside the cathedral it seemed as if Tom had completed for us what Anne and I had been unable to do. And who knows, Tom may have other paths to tread in the future, and maybe even a book to write.

Each one of us, I believe, is constantly being called to follow the path which will lead us to eternal life. Jesus is The Way, and like the good shepherd that He is, He will constantly call us back when we stray. In life, some will stray from the path, some will never leave it, others will criss-cross it throughout their lives whilst others are yet to begin their spiritual journey. Each person's experience is unique, but God is patient, waiting for the day when we finally listen for His voice and follow His way.

As for me, I continue to prepare for when my earthly life arrives at Journey's End and I will hopefully meet our Heavenly Father and be re-united with my beloved husband, Tom.

My dearest hope is that if you, too, in reading my accounts have been encouraged, challenged or redirected in your life in any way, that you will have the courage to cooperate with that 'still small voice' within and go on listening! You may be pleasantly surprised!

AUTHOR'S BIOGRAPHY

Pauline Doyle was born in Manchester and received a good Catholic education. Despite being a high achiever, she left school at sixteen to help support her disabled mother. At fifty, she returned to study and undertook a course in Pastoral Theology at The Maria Assumpta Centre, Kensington. Following this qualification, she was invited to study two modules of an MA Religious Studies course focusing on adult learning at St Mary's University, Twickenham. She then accepted her Diocesan Director of Education's invitation to train parish leaders.

Pauline later qualified as a professional counsellor and practised for several years, at the same time as caring for her beloved husband, Tom, after he suffered a major stroke. When not writing, Pauline follows the various pursuits of her loving and gifted children and grandchildren.